# Chanticleer

# Chanticleer

## A Pleasure Garden

ADRIAN HIGGINS

Photographs by ROB CARDILLO

PENN

UNIVERSITY OF PENNSYLVANIA PRESS

PHILADELPHIA

FRONTISPIECE *In and around the forecourt, autumn is a season to crow about. Weeks after their initial flowering, the* Hydrangea serrata *'Preziosa' turn to claret against the yellow foliage of the 'Accolade' cherries.*

Published by
University of Pennsylvania Press
Philadelphia, Pennsylvania 19104-4112
www.upenn.edu/pennpress

Printed in Canada on acid-free paper
10 9 8 7 6 5 4 3 2 1

BOOK DESIGN & COMPOSITION: Judith Stagnitto Abbate / Abbate Design

Library of Congress Cataloging-in-Publication Data

Higgins, Adrian.
  Chanticleer : a pleasure garden / Adrian Higgins ; photographs by Rob Cardillo.
— 1st ed.
    p. cm.
  ISBN 978-0-8122-4274-4 (hardcover : alk. paper)
  1. Chanticleer Gardens (Wayne, Pa.) 2. Gardens—Pennsylvania—Wayne.  I.
Cardillo, Rob.
  SB466.U7H54 2011
  712'.60974814—dc22
                        2010039356

# Contents

This book is a testament to the people who have made Chanticleer. To Adolph and Christine Rosengarten, who purchased the property, built the home, and raised two children who would grow up to love the place. To their son, Adolph, Jr., who loved the trees, lawns, homes, and spirit of the site so much he left it to be a public garden. He endowed it well and trusted the Board of Directors he appointed and the staff he and they hired to develop the property into something special. To his wife, Janet, who tended her own personal flower garden outside her husband's library window and advised him to preserve the land, inspiring the Foundation's creation.

To the members of the Board of Directors, who manage the money wisely, set policies carefully, who love the garden enough to trust its operation to a skilled and talented staff, and who know each employee's name. To Christopher Woods, Chanticleer's first Executive Director, who transformed a pretty estate into an amazing pleasure garden. And, finally, to the staff, who have designed the garden, made it visually and sensually exciting, and built the furniture, the bridges, and the drinking fountains.

On his first visit to the gardens, writer Adrian Higgins understood Chanticleer. He recognized its liveliness, and he comprehended the artistry and continual reinvention of the site. He witnessed the love and devotion the staff incorporates into every aspect of the place. He visited regularly and spoke with each person. He has ably conveyed into words the uniqueness of Chanticleer.

Rob Cardillo has photographed Chanticleer for many years now. He enthusiastically embraced this project, capturing a year in images. Living nearby, he came whenever the light was just right, the garden at the stage he wanted. I would often see him while I was on an early morning or late afternoon walk. He was tenacious about capturing a particular image and with his inquisitive eye he has made many stunning views of the garden.

Accurately encapsulating a garden in words and images is an agreeable but daunting task —and nearly im-possible. A garden is multidimensional, having visual and textural depth complemented with sounds and smells. It is an ephemeral place, changing daily, with plants coming into and out of bloom, and by the moment, as the sun goes behind a cloud, a breeze blows, a bird chirps. For this difficult task, we have two amazing artists to portray the garden. Welcome to Chanticleer!

R. WILLIAM THOMAS,
*Executive Director and Head Gardener*

# Chanticleer

# Chanticleer

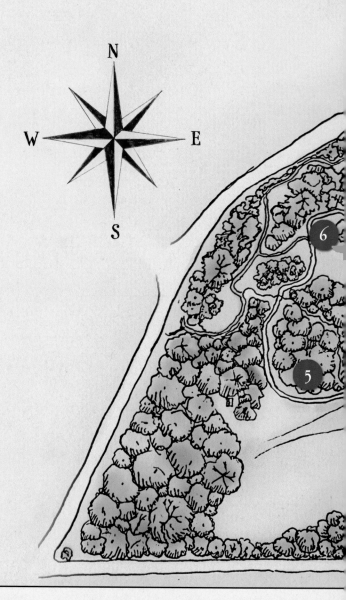

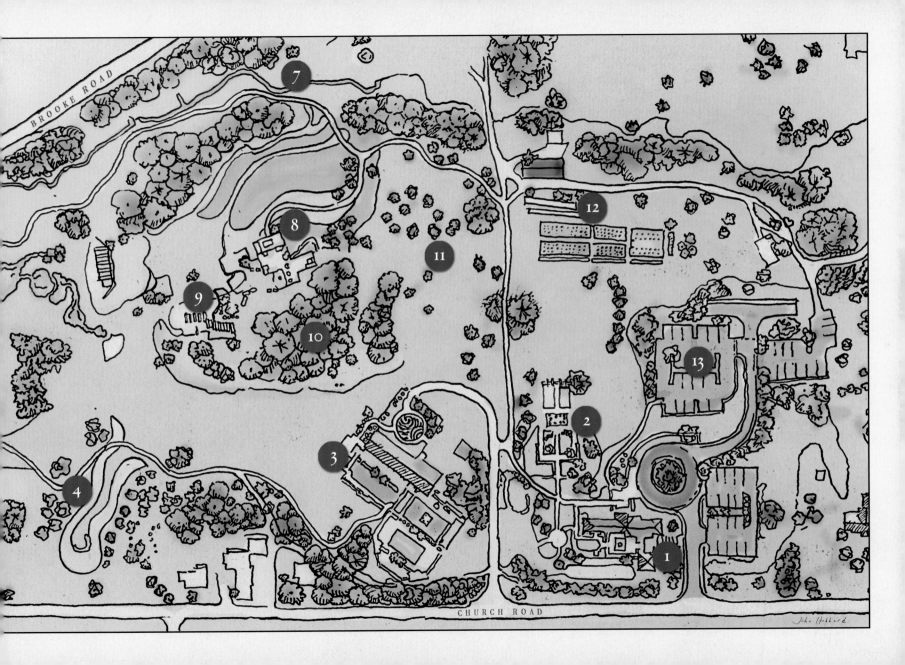

BROOKE ROAD

CHURCH ROAD

7

8

9

10

11

12

13

3

2

1

4

John Hubbard

# The Meaning of Chanticleer

This book took me from my home in Alexandria, Virginia, to Chanticleer Garden on Philadelphia's Main Line many times over two growing seasons. I had known the garden since 2000 and sensed then that the dynamics at play were producing a place quite unlike any other I had seen in twenty-five years of garden writing. So when I returned repeatedly for this project, I rejoiced at the prospect of getting to know Chanticleer Garden far more deeply, not just in its horticultural topography, but in the way that it changed from month to month, even week to week. That sounds too passive—it changes because of the endless toil and imagination of some exceedingly talented horticulturists under the direction of Bill Thomas, a plantsman, designer, and manager of the highest standards and expectations. Together they have created a magical landscape of invention and reinvention.

For me as an observer, there were moments of sheer bliss, unexpectedly in the pale drizzle of early spring, when the magnolias and cherry trees sparkled far off through the mist. And what business had the exotic echiums blooming in April and May in the shivering rain? There were a few laughs, too, notably when a gentleman came to the

*Sunken and winding Bell's Run is given elevation in late April and early May, when thousands of camassias form a corresponding stream.*

entrance kiosk and asked to be directed to "the flowers." There were flowers all about, and blooms add vital interest to the experience, but Chanticleer isn't about flowers alone; it's about plants, plants on their stage. It's music, it's ballet, it's cinema. It's the garden as an art form, and in the twenty years of active garden making here, Chanticleer has developed an international reputation among those in the know as one of the most theatrical gardens in the United States. But it's a refined theater; the horticulture is inherently sophisticated, and for those who need to know the plants they are viewing it can be a challenging one, too.

Chanticleer is smaller than many other horticultural institutions, and the multilayering of the spaces, the plantings, and the design elements give it a heady intensity. But it's not just the density of the plantings. The institutional culture here is different from other places, in part because of Chanticleer's size but also because of the unorthodox ethos established by the first executive director, Chris Woods, and enriched further by Bill Thomas. Large public gardens tend to be conservative, averse to risks, and in these places new garden installations are the product of many layers of deliberation and approval. The gardeners on the ground may often be charged with implementing planting schemes and designs not of their making.

The culture at Chanticleer is quite the opposite. To extend the performance metaphor, at Chanticleer the seven horticulturists and craftsman are the artists under the direction of Thomas (and, on a strategic level, the garden's board of directors). The ideas are generated from the bottom up, to be considered, guided, perhaps modified or even rejected, by Thomas. Major projects go to the board for approval and funding. This approach is only feasible, of course, if you have a select band of gardeners. "They have to perform well, but it's almost effortless to them because they do it so well," said Thomas. The pressure is on, constantly, and yet, he says, "I don't think they feel it. But they know they have to do a great job. We can't settle for good."

One of Thomas's other accomplishments is the purchase of a ten-acre tract to protect the view across Church Road. It otherwise would have held a large house as part of the subdivision of what was once the eight-hundred-acre estate of Ardrossan, the opulent home of Helen Hope Montgomery Scott (1904–1995). She was the glamorous Main Line heiress who was the model for Tracy Lord in

*The Philadelphia Story,* played in its original Broadway run, as well as in the 1940 film version, by Katharine Hepburn. The garden occupies thirty-five of Chanticleer's amassed forty-seven acres in a rough triangle bounded by Church Road to the south and curving Brooke Road to the north and west.

Chanticleer Garden owes its origin to one man's devotion to his family's estate in Wayne, Pennsylvania, and his desire for it to become an exceptional public garden. It is safe to say that Adolph Rosengarten, Jr. (1905–1990) rests in peace. He first came here in 1913, when his parents, Adolph Rosengarten, Sr., and Emily Christine Penrose Rosengarten, built the main house as a country retreat from Philadelphia. When their daughter, Emily, married in 1935, they built the adjoining mansion on Church Road, now the first building visitors encounter. When Adolph Jr. had married two years earlier, his parents bought a neighboring house and sold it to the newlyweds for $1. This was

*Mr. Rosengarten, Jr. on his way to the stables. Probably taken while he was stationed overseas at Bletchley Park in the 1940s.*

in the depths of the Great Depression. The family, you will have gathered, was wealthy.

The Rosengarten forebears, German immigrants, had created a pharmaceutical company in Philadelphia that would later merge with Merck to become one of the largest drug companies in the world. Young Adolph was informed by his father that the family needed a lawyer, and so he took a degree in law. When America entered World War II, he first joined the Pennsylvania National Guard and later transferred to military intelligence and an assignment to Bletchley Park. This was the country estate northwest of London where the Allies cracked the Enigma code, whose revelation would become a vital element in the defeat of Nazi Germany.

In the picturesque countryside of suburban London, Rosengarten would have seen and appreciated many majestic old trees. In those days centuries-old elms formed long allées radiating from country houses. They have since fallen to Dutch elm disease. Perhaps one cool October morning he was pondering his work and looked up to see a horse chestnut tree in its orange glory and thought of the Ohio buckeye back home, and of its own singular beauty.

Adolph Rosengarten, Jr., loved trees, and the cultural legacy of Chanticleer that he and his sister, and their parents before them, left for us was dependent on trees in what was once open farmland. Without them today, Chanticleer would lose its air of permanence and be seen for what it is: essentially a remarkable but young garden begun in 1990. There is little record of who planted the trees, or when, but it is safe to say that most of them do not predate the family's settlement here in 1913. This was a place for crops and not heavily forested.

But the path extending northward from the Chanticleer House gate used to be a farm road and has four surviving members of an avenue of black walnut trees thought to have been planted in the 1870s, and nearby stands a towering Norway spruce, which was the family's live Christmas tree in 1917. The cutting garden is marked by a couple of old katsura trees of uncertain age. The spreading tree is male, the upright one female. The oak overlook-

*The deeply fissured bark of the native black walnut serves as a decorative reminder of Chanticleer's agrarian origins.*

ing the Tennis Court Garden was planted sometime in the mid-1930s and is a naturally occurring hybrid between the white oak and the chestnut oak. Like many of the treasured trees on the estate, it has extensive lightning protection. A copper cable extends from conductors high in the tree to a rod buried in the ground several feet from the base of the trunk. The magnificent red oak tree in the Minder Woods area of Chanticleer was saved by such a device in the late 1980s. The morning after a fierce electrical storm, gardeners noticed a hole in the soil near the rod; turf and soil had been sent flying, but the tree was unscathed.

Peter Brindle, who is the grounds manager and worked for Rosengarten when he lived in Minder House, is struck by the sophistication of his tree planting. Rosengarten, whom he still calls "Mr. R," planted underused, beautiful native trees such as tupelos, yellowwoods, and sourwoods, and choice exotics like the Oriental spruce and cutleaf European beech. "He loved native trees, fine trees, and his legacy was in planting loads of wonderful trees around the garden and creating terrific vistas and views," said Brindle.

One of the most astonishing things, however, is how quickly the silver linden next to the overlook of Chanticleer House has matured. It was planted in the early 1990s, replacing a sycamore that was lost, and now looks many decades old, with a beautifully rounded canopy.

Rosengarten wanted Chanticleer to become a public garden, and in the 1970s he consulted prominent horticultural and institutional experts in the Delaware Valley, including Richard Lighty, then of Longwood Gardens in Kennett Square, Pennsylvania, Paul Meyer of the Morris Arboretum in Philadelphia, the landscape designer William H. Frederick, and Ernesta Ballard of the Pennsylvania Horticultural Society. In time his thinking changed, and he saw Chanticleer not as the arboretum that he first envisioned but as a place that embraced a fuller expression of ornamental horticulture. He once listed as his models Sissinghurst Castle and Bodnant, two of Britain's finest gardens.

Slowly his vision of Chanticleer took shape. He assembled neighboring properties, and the foundation he cre-

*By the side of an old farm road near the Cutting Garden, a pair of venerable katsura trees turn golden in October.*

ated would gather more, so that what was once a ten-acre property became forty-seven acres. He had an established gardening staff that included the brothers Luther and Rush Dalton, who worked at Chanticleer for decades, and during Rosengarten's absence in World War II they decided that they would build stone walls to channel Bell's Run, a stream at the edge of the estate. The beauty of their work endures.

In 1983 Rosengarten hired a young English gardener named Chris Woods, who had been trained at the Royal Botanical Gardens, Kew. This would prove momentous. Woods, who in 1990 became Chanticleer's first executive director, formulated a clear vision of how the garden should develop, assembled a team of highly talented horticulturists, and gave them the freedom to be creative and take risks.

I was thinking of this when I was with Douglas Randolph, the farmer in charge of agricultural crops in the Serpentine area of Chanticleer, in the early summer of 2009. A couple of weeks before, he had planted hundreds of cotton seedlings that not only seemed stalled but were afflicted badly by thrips and aphids. Randolph didn't know

whether to spray or employ predator insects against them, deciding on the latter. "I hope it works," he said. "It's a little bit of a worry." Of course, by the end of August, the cotton had grown perfectly.

A year earlier, Chanticleer horticulturist Dan Benarcik was putting in a plant scheme in the terraced beds behind Chanticleer House that included a tender shrub called *Coprosma*. He hadn't tried it before and was worried about coprosma's reputation for not doing well in hot humid weather. Chanticleer doesn't have a production greenhouse, so the gardeners don't have access to mature backup plants to plug in midseason. The coprosma grew happily, as it turned out, but at the time Benarcik said: "It's either going to be amazing or a colossal failure. There's an expression we used to use with Chris, gardening without a net."

This captures perfectly what's going on at Chanticleer: it's a horticultural high-wire act.

Few of the plants are labeled, and this no doubt frustrates some visitors. Chanticleer spends a lot of effort keeping plant lists up to date and available in the various garden areas. The philosophy is that once you label everything, the place shifts from being a garden to a classroom. Labels draw the eye and stop the feet and would make the journey through Chanticleer much more halting and distracted. And although Chanticleer's mission is to inspire visitors in their own gardening, the principal role of a pleasure garden is enjoyment.

A great deal of thought and knowledge and toil—and yes, money—have made Chanticleer what it is, but the visitor is not meant to be burdened by that. "Garden making is fundamentally not an intellectual enterprise," Woods told me once. "Most people come to gardens to experience some form of beauty."

The first years were marked by frenetic creation. The orchard meadow alone has a hundred thousand daffodil bulbs, after an initial planting of forty thousand in 1991. Asian Woods was retrieved from a forest thick with weeds. The Pond Garden was dug out of a hillside. During the tenure of Bill Thomas, the gardens have been refined and enlarged and have reached a measure of equilibrium that comes with maturity. But the high-wire act continues.

The horticulturists meet at 7:30 A.M. on Mondays to announce their plans for the week, which might be any-

*Adolph Rosengarten, Jr., clipping the Chanticleer hedges in June 1954 while his nephew, O. P. Jackson, Jr. looks on.*

thing from extra weeding after a gardener's absence to the protection of tender plants against a possible frost. In the fall individual gardeners begin to bounce off Thomas their ideas for the next season. And during the year Thomas works with the gardeners in refining the plantings. A stand of ornamental grass might have become too large for its design; certain beds might need a clearer connection to each other with plants that sustain forms and colors. Thomas generally sees each of the horticulturists in his or her area every couple of days. In highly dynamic areas such as the Chanticleer House terraces, he and Dan Benarcik will review the plantings carefully every two weeks to see, Thomas said, "what the display is looking like, what he's happy with, what I'm happy with, what we are not happy with."

The photographs in this book show clearly that Chanticleer Garden is not one garden. It provides a breadth of horticultural experiences that matches its depth. It is a native garden, an exotic garden, a shade garden, a sun garden, a rock garden, an aquatic garden, a container garden, a tropical garden, a wild garden. It is a garden of follies and sculptures and handcrafted bridges and benches. It is a garden that exists in time as well as space, from the moment

*Corn poppies and verbascum frame a darkening June sky gathering above the west end of Chanticleer House.*

the *Edgeworthia* opens on the Chanticleer House rear terrace in late March to the days in late October when the sourwoods of Minder Woods turn deep burgundy. Amid this immense diversity, however, there is the thread of perfection entwined with whimsy. Brindle remembers Rosengarten as a courtly gentleman of the old school, and a creature of habit. In summer he would swim in the pool every day at noon. When it snowed, the grounds crews would plow paths around the garden so that he could still take his daily constitutional. He would pay his staff bonuses on their birthdays and holidays, and he would also slip them a packet when they returned from their vacations. That may have seemed counterintuitive, but Rosengarten knew, Brindle said, that "nobody is as broke as when they come back from vacation. What a thoughtful thing. I thought I was seeing the last of a breed."

Rosengarten's impulse to enlarge and preserve the estate was driven in part by the loss of the countryside in the Main Line to development, particularly shopping malls, and since to the paradox of subdivisions of mansions. By contrast, four valuable houses, including his own, would

be removed for the sake of the garden. That's something to ponder. The gardeners often wonder what he would make of their efforts in the twenty-first century. He once cautioned against a garden that was so elaborate it would be impossible for visitors to emulate. I think Chris Woods took a different approach and felt that, above all else, this was a garden where one should lose oneself in a floral paradise.

Peter Brindle thinks about this a lot. Rosengarten, he said, "would be taken aback, and maybe a little horrified at first. And then I think he would be thrilled."

What we do know is that Rosengarten established an institution that has elevated the cause of horticulture in America. It is comforting to realize that one can spend a couple of hours in Chanticleer and be uplifted by its floral alchemy, even if we don't know all the plants by name. As Rosengarten himself said, "Gardening is the most wonderful way of refreshing yourself."

I spoke earlier of reinvention. In a garden of such virtuosity and variety, it is imperative that the displays change from year to year, especially in the most fluid gardens, the Teacup and Entry Gardens, the Chanticleer House terrac-

es, and the Cutting Garden, with their emphasis on container plantings, tropicals, and annuals. Even something as seemingly static as Asian Woods changes, from the subtle realignment of paths to the addition of nooks and crannies for sitting and the reworking of some plant groupings.

And so it is the directives to the gardeners, spoken and implicit, that underlie the essence of Chanticleer—be brilliant, be inventive, and do something fresh next year. Neither a museum nor a great plodding institution, Chanticleer is a gardener's garden.

---
| CHAPTER 1 |
---

# Teacup and Entry Gardens

*Five houses sit on the entire forty-seven-acre Chanticleer estate, six if you count the Ruin, where Chanticleer's benefactor, Adolph Rosengarten, Jr., once had a perfectly unruined home. But it is the*

grand house of his sister, Emily Rosengarten, that welcomes visitors and sets the whole mood for the Chanticleer experience. The senior Rosengartens built it for her when she married a lumber importer named Samuel Goodman in 1935; Goodman died just eleven years later, at the age of thirty-nine. After her death Adolph Rosengarten, Jr., pur-

chased the house from her second husband, O. P. Jackson, Sr., in 1983.

Today the house is used as an administration building, and, more important for the garden, it is the visitor's first experience of Chanticleer and sets both the tone and the standard for the entire garden. The house, essentially, is a

*The west end of the house overlooks the Oak Bed. The tree on the right corner is* Acer negundo *'Kelly's Gold'.*

stage on which the plants perform. The warm gray stuccoed fabric of the mansion is a perfect passive backdrop for the horticulture. The architecture exudes an air of Mediterranean serenity, especially as the bananas, taros, and other tropicals take form in the heat of early summer.

The displays occupy all sides of the house in traditional beds and borders and in an extravagant array of containers. Hardy and tender, native and exotic plants revel in an exuberant celebration. The garden achieves for the plant kingdom what Noah's Ark accomplished for the animals, but without the clouds.

The containers are planted with a spring palette that takes the gardens through the first eight weeks of the season and then replanted with warm-season plants that have given the Teacup and Entry Gardens their wide reputation as a tropical display of surpassing quality and innovation. Indeed, for a while the Teacup Garden was called the Tropical Teacup, but Bill Thomas dropped the "tropical" label because it suggested that's all it was, and, of course, it was and is so much more than that.

*Garden entrance.*

In their cool-blooded spring incarnation, the container plantings still achieve the daring and exotic mood of the later tropical material, proving that in the hands of an artful designer, it's not the material that matters but how you use it. A visitor on a misty, cool morning in April—OK, so there are some clouds—might find a forty-two-inch clay pot, four feet from rim to floor, with a living arrangement of purples (a young shrub of maroon-leafed, purple-blossomed *Loropetalum chinense* 'Zhuzhou Fuchsia', 'Bright Lights Mix' chard, 'Bull's Blood' beet, Excelsior Hybrids foxglove) and violet-blue (*Saponaria ocymoides* and an unnamed hybrid of wallflower, *Erysimum*).

From the first cool stirrings of spring in early April to the first wash of warm, humid air in mid-May, the temperate character of these gardens changes almost daily. The first visitors of the season find the north border open and quiet except for a magnificent *Corylopsis sinensis,* whose pale yellow flowers fill the air with sweet perfume, but once it fades, its bedfellows, hydrangeas, hostas, an *Acer*

*Excelsior Hybrids foxglove is taken from its woodland shadows to center stage, where it is exalted.*

*olivarianum* ssp. *olivarianum,* swiftly vegetate the scene. Similarly, by the entrance pavilion, a bank of variegated Solomon's seal pushes up horns of light maroon that within a week grow into a mass of stems, eventually festooned with creamy white bell-like flowers on one side, directing the lengthening stems where to arch. May brings lush and immaculate vegetation. The garden, so naked a month before, is now captured in verdant perfection.

On the other side of the house, the transformation is similarly stark, but here the upper terrace is dominated by a daffodil lawn, framed by the thick, peeling trunks of the Heritage ('Cully') river birch, still out of leaf. The view down this narcissus boulevard is terminated at the focal point of a variegated American agave on a pedestal. This juxtaposition of a moody and huge sub-tropic-al succulent with cheery northern-clime daffodils is not so much jarring as simply unexpected. The pairing

*In the bed below the curving retaining wall of the entrance circle, the blossoms of the Asian redbud,* Cercis gigantea, *erupt in April and later form striking seed pods borne on the stems like seaweed on a rock.*

brings tension and thus drama. It is the quintessence of Chanticleer.

As the daffodil 'Honeybird' fades, the evergreen *Euphorbia amygdaloides* var. *robbiae* blooms acid green and generally perks up from its frost-battered state. The upper terrace has two lovely kousa dogwoods, now with broad canopies that speak to the flowering dogwood on the terrace below. All three dogwoods are draped with *Schizophragma integrifolium,* a hydrangea vine whose smooth bark, varnished by the spring rain, resembles a snake making its way through its hosts' branches, particularly on the flowering dogwood. On the retaining wall behind the flowering dogwood, the hydrangea makes its own way in the shade of the tree.

The climbing hydrangea and the schizophragma are closely related and often confused, so their juxtaposition here offers a study in both their similarities and their differences. The leaves of the climbing hydrangea are small and

*In an edible phase, Swiss chard meets peppers and trailing rosemary.*

thick and ruffled, and its aerial lacecaps produce showy outer sterile flowers or rays, a ring of white four-leafed clovers. The schizophragma, by contrast, has larger, flat leaves that are much more heart-shaped. The outer lacecap flowers are lone and paddle-shaped. *Schizophragma integrifolium* also has bigger and flatter leaves than the more commonly planted *Schizophragma hydrangeoides,* which can be seen on the north side of the house. The hydrangea blooms in the middle of May, the schizophragma about two weeks later. Both deciduous vines take several years to produce their first blooms, but once mature, as here, they are free-flowering. Gardener Jonathan Wright trims them so that the blossoms remain within the heart of the dogwoods and don't compete with the trees' own lovely white blossoms.

The Teacup Garden is named after the central fountain behind the house. Family lore has it that Christine Penrose Rosengarten picked up the concrete fountain on a trip to

*The glorious season overture on the Upper Border, masses of Narcissus 'Honeybird' before the variegated American agave.*

The blue-green cast of the variegated American agave matches
the weathered copper pot it's in.

Lettuce 'Red Sails' beneath the Pati palm, Syagrus botryophora.

Florence in the 1920s. Originally on the terrace above the swimming pool at Chanticleer House, it was moved to its current site in the early 1990s.

The cup's four falling streams of water give voice to the space. This liquid quartet sings constantly through the season, but the flora beneath it change from spring to summer and year to year. One year, Wright decided to explore the beauty of edible plants, and the Teacup Bed became a victory garden of sorts. After the decorative lettuce and mustard greens grew big in May and then erupted into flower, he planted a golden-leafed sweet potato and pineapples whose fruit, familiar and yet so unfamiliar on the plant, swelled in the summer heat.

Earlier, the nascent lettuce was laid out in rows, through which the dainty flowers of a white and yellow *Linaria* and the bolder, golden daisies of *Osteospermum* Lemon Symphony ('Seikilrem') danced like sprites in the gathering sunshine of spring.

One of the most enlightening aspects of this experiment was the planting of papaya trees, which go from seed in the greenhouse in April to serious young trees in August. A plant overwintered one year in the greenhouse has a thick, woody trunk and is stuffed with the melon-sized fruit in its second summer. For a tree, it goes about its business quickly, and then dies. But what a show.

In late winter, the gardener harvests canes of the yellowtwig dogwood from the Parking Lot Garden and arranges them in overlapping arcs as a perimeter fence for the Teacup Bed. The idea is to create a decorative barrier against tiny feet, but within a few weeks the contorted stems have not only pushed new leafy growth, but are presenting the odd white blossom or two. Thus simple twigs become a metaphor for the fecundity of this place. As summer reaches its zenith the south-facing Teacup Garden becomes hot and bright, and the task is to bring some cooling effects, not just in the canopy of this transplanted jungle,

*In this Teacup planting, an underlying cool theme of blues and whites is enlivened with the sherbet hues of the Iceland poppy,* Papaver nudicaule. *The* Agave americana *is underplanted with the* Festuca glauca *'Elijah Blue', and the poppies are mixed with* Cerastium tomentosum *and the yellow spikes of* Asphodeline lutea.

*In the Lower Courtyard, the flowering dogwood branch veils red Abyssinian bananas,* Ensete vetricosum *'Maurelii'. In the foreground is a young pink velvet banana,* Musa velutina, *a bromeliad,* Alcantarea imperialis, *and the red leaf Brazilian tree fern,* Blechnum brasiliense *'Crispum'. The blue-flowered sweet pea,* Lathyrus odoratus, *offers the last of its season's blooms.*

Cotinus coggygria *'Velvet Cloak' with bronze fennel.*

but through the use of chilling colors such as blues and silvers. This is achieved in some years with the fanlike fronds of the palm *Bismarckia nobilis* (silver blue), *Agave gentryi* 'Jaws' (minty green but baring teeth), and *Agave attenuata* (silver green), as well as the blue flowers of *Agapanthus campanulatus.* The sound of the fountain bounces around the semienclosed space, doing its bit to cool the garden. The odd splash of hot color, however, keeps the experience on edge, and may be achieved with something as delicate as a sowing of the annual *Emilia coccinea,* whose delicate orange-red flowers are borne on wiry stems.

Chanticleer sits on the cold edge of plant hardiness zone 7, but along the south-facing wall of the Teacup Garden, exotic plants have come to ignore this designation. Here, Jonathan Wright has planted such absurdly tender things as callas, the aforementioned agapanthus, and the palm *Sabal minor,* which was once thought to limit its northern reaches to North Carolina. A glossy-leafed

*The dainty, thistle like bloom of* Emilia coccinea, *a willing annual often used in the Teacup Bed.*

schefflera, *Schefflera delavayi*— yes, a relative of the house plant—grows here and sends up white flowers reminiscent of goatsbeard.

The Kitchen Courtyard is one of the most cosseting spaces at Chanticleer, cozily intimate and brought to life with containers filled with captivating plant combinations. One year there were succulents, and in glaucous grays and pinks, in troughs of extraordinary architecture. When he chose the veggie theme, Jonathan Wright used purple-leafed cabbages that appeared to have been fashioned by a blacksmith, including one sitting high on the entrance wall. How did he water it, how did he keep the cabbage worms off it? These are among the imponderables of Chanticleer.

Summer and fall are unabashed celebrations of tropical plants, one year in the Lower Courtyard the arrowhead and deeply veined leaves of the *Colocasia* (Thai Giant Strain) reached six feet from base to tip. The big blue bottlebrush flowers of the container plantings

*The Abyssinian banana,* Ensete ventricosum *'Maurelii'. Its rootball is lifted and stored each winter.*

*The Oak Bed in spring, a delicious mix of woodland perennials painstakingly planted to avoid root damage. The purple shrub is* Weigela florida *'Foliis Purpureus'.*

# CHAPTER 2

# Tennis Court Garden

*The vestigial rectangle of a tennis court, once bounded by thick hemlocks, today provides one of the most geometric gardens at Chanticleer, and with it the opportunity to temper straight lines*

with soft plantings. That contrast is one of many pleasing paradoxes about this garden, and it comes into play as soon as you move through the transitional beds away from the Teacup Garden to the broad shoulders of the upper beds at the top of the stairs to the Tennis Court Garden.

The duality of the space is first experienced at the top of the entrance stairs. The visitor stops, instinctively, to look down on what is a view garden. In April there is another arresting factor here, the thick perfume of the delicate white and pink blossoms of the variegated *Daphne × burkwoodii* 'Carol Mackie'. In another age, or in another style, the urge might have been to install a knot garden or parterre where the court had once been and have it function solely as a sort of huge floral rug, to be seen from

*When April is still young and cool, the redbud reigns over burgeoning beds and coordinated drifts of tulips.*

above. Mercifully, we are spared that, because the second and more important role of the garden is to have the visitor in it. One steps down the stone stairs to enjoy the mix of perennials, shrubs, bulbs, and annuals in the five central beds. Once you have descended, the idea of a single view disappears. New views unfurl, framed by walls and banks and trees, and one revels with the plants in a comforting sense of enclosure.

The walls of the stairway are actually planters, and one gets a notion that the gardener is having entirely too much fun. The plant combinations vary, but have consisted in the past of lamb's ears planted in combination with the hop marjoram (*Origanum dictamnus*), named for its mauve, hoplike inflorescence. In an early-season planting, the gardener combined grape hyacinths with apricot-colored violas, purple mustard greens, and *Hyacinthus orientalis* 'Blue Festival'.

The five central beds of the Tennis Court Garden have

*The stair walls, with their planters, bring a succession of playful and tactile plant combinations that change through the seasons and years.*

been revamped in recent years. Where once the beds featured their own color schemes, they have been reworked extensively so that they are singing not so much to each other as in a chorus. Shrubs and dwarf conifers, while still important elements, have been reduced to bring in a richer mix of plants. You might call it a melting pot, so eclectic and unexpected the assortment, from a native catalpa tree (cultivar 'Aurea') coppiced as a perennial in March to keep it in bounds and enlarge the leaves, to the cape-fuchsia, *Phygelius,* which has proven perfectly hardy in this enclave.

Given the variety of the material, it became important to establish planting schemes that were coherent in themselves but also linked to neighboring beds. This has been achieved in two basic ways: with a series of carefully planned peaks of bloom and foliage, and with a planting design that provides not only plant repetitions from bed to bed, but also ribbons of color and textures that run through the beds. The five central beds are deceptively large. Together they occupy an area of 3,160 square feet, and if they were reordered as a linear border 12 feet deep, it would stretch for more than 260 feet.

The first peak is achieved with tulips, mostly Triumph

*Like a chick emerging from its shell, the florets of* Allium hollandicum *'Purple Sensation' race to greet the world.*

types, in saturated colors. A combination of rich reds, purples, and golden tulips might well consist of rivers of 'Bastogne' (blood red), 'Negrita' (deep purple), 'Golden Parade' (buttercup yellow), 'Queen of Night' (black-purple), and 'Recreado' (purple-wine). They bloom just as the deciduous magnolias close to the arbor (*Magnolia* 'Jane' and *M. liliiflora* 'O'Neill') begin to leaf out and slowly shed their gorgeous purple floral chalices. The large and showy redbud 'Forest Pansy' is in full sail with the tulips, which flower for a couple of weeks when all the herbaceous plants are pushing a lot of growth. Perhaps the most striking is the specimen of Chinese rhubarb, *Rheum palmatum* var. *tanguticum.* Its large palmate leaves emerge upright to reveal lower surfaces of striking red venation. The tulips and trees are not alone in providing eye-popping color so early. Several high-octane spurges ignite the beds with chrome yellow drifts, including the *Euphorbia polychroma* cultivars 'Bonfire' and 'Candy'.

The next peak occurs soon afterward, in early May, when the alliums, Siberian irises, and herbaceous peonies try to outdo each other. Among the ornamental onions are *Allium nigrum,* which in spite of its name flowers white or faint lilac (*nigrum* derives from its near-black ovaries); *A.* 'Purple Sensation', tall and showy, with a flower head that is a rich violet-purple; *A.* 'Globemaster', whose enormous purple floral sphere makes this onion a showboat; and *A.* 'Gladiator', another impossibly flashy purple-robed allium.

They flower with *Iris sibirica* 'Berlin Purple Wine', large, velvety, and of the deepest purple wine color; *I. sibirica* 'Dancing Nanou', a clear purple with handsome venation; and the redder varieties, 'Eric the Red' and 'Ruby Wine', whose red-violet shifts the color pitch and links to the *Paeonia* 'Scarlet O'Hara', which is a large single red with golden anthers. The showiest of the herbaceous peonies is 'Big Ben', a large, double-flowered cultivar with deep magenta pink blooms. It was hybridized by an Amer-

*As the tulips recede, hundreds of allium varieties appear to continue the interlocking motif between the five central beds. The shorter, darker onion is* Allium hollandicum *'Purple Sensation', the taller lighter purple one is* Allium *'Gladiator'. The drumsticks provide a complementary hue to the vibrant red and gold spring growth of the* Spiraea × bumalda *'Magic Carpet'.*

ican grower, Edward Auten, Jr. (1881–1974), known for his work on red cultivars. The peony world continues to evolve.

'Bartzella' is an amazing clear yellow, double-flowered peony cultivar and a member of a new hybrid form between the herbaceous and tree peony. The offspring of woody and herbaceous species is an oddity in horticulture, but these hybrids have been met with extraordinary excitement among peony aficionados. The herbaceous peony, while a stalwart of the American garden, presents its own difficulties, especially in the warm mid-Atlantic region. The high petal count of so many herbaceous varieties makes them incredibly showy, but also prone to diseases and stresses that prevent the buds from reaching maturity. When they do open, they can be too heavy for the stems and flop, or get beaten down in a heavy rain. In many years, precociously hot weather in May causes them to fade quickly. The tree peonies do not suffer these problems, and they tend to bloom a month before the herbaceous ones, when it is still decidedly cool. The hybrids, which are known as intersectional peonies, function as herbaceous peonies in that their top growth withers in the fall, but in season they look more like tree peonies in foliage and bloom. The flowers are more open than spherical, and the thick stems hold them aloft through thick and thin. They bloom soon after the tree peonies, but successively, and the display is long and glorious.

By early summer the herbaceous plantings of the Tennis Court are so full that the garden takes on a mantle that it wears until frost, one in which the textures and forms of the vegetation play off each other. But floral color remains a key element, and in July the focus shifts to lilies, red hot pokers (kniphofias), and crocosmias. Among the lilies are the lovely species *Lilium hansonii*, with its nodding and fragrant turk's-caps, the tiger lily, *L. lancifolium*, and the particularly striking *L. nepalense*, whose petal tips of faint yellow-green contrast dramatically with throats of mahogany red. One of the crocosmia cultivars is the ever-popular 'Lucifer', with large flame-red flowers. The crocosmias offer arching sprays of flowers, and the red hot pokers provide glorious exclamation marks—even the diminutive species *Kniphofia citrina*, growing to just twelve inches with an ivory-colored inflorescence. By contrast, *K.* 'Alcazar' is tall and screams an orange-red hue.

Dominated as it is by hardy herbaceous plants, the Tennis Court Garden is one of the most dynamic compositions at Chanticleer. Through the season it evolves, its character changing from a demure, almost hesitant celebration of early spring to a revelry in high summer that borders on sizzling hedonism. It is telling that when hobbyist photographers arrive at Chanticleer they seem to make a beeline to the Tennis Court Garden, where they find the microcosmic beauty of flower details but also a framework that will enhance their picture compositions.

In late summer the garden is given structure with contrasting ribbons of grasses, the first the stiff and upright *Calamagrostis* × *acutiflora* 'Karl Foerster' and the softer, wispy switchgrass *Panicum virgatum* 'Shenandoah'. 'Karl Foerster' is one of those rare plants whose familiarity does

*In late summer, the dahlia 'Mystic Desire' provides drama against the foliage ornament of the red-veined dock,* Rumex sanguineus.

By the fall, the garden has lost the floral edge of spring, replaced by the softer beauty of leaves and stems, backlit by the declining sun.

# CHAPTER 3

# Chanticleer House

*Wayne is one of a string of towns along the old Pennsylvania Railroad's Main Line. Before the age of the automobile, the train service gave Philadelphia's wealthiest families access to a region where*

they could build large country houses in rolling pastures and leafy woods, away from the heat and insalubrious bustle of the city. It was a social place where the wealthy could both associate with their own lofty ilk and engage in the sport of competitive conspicuous consumption. It should be said, though, that among such districts in the United States the Main Line stands out for the relative restraint of the style and scale of its domestic architecture, and its houses certainly make what passes for a new mansion in our own age a temple to feigned cultivation.

Adolph Rosengarten, Sr., undoubtedly knew the area well when he and his wife, Christine, chose to build a

*Terrace beds and container plantings form a floral wonderland in the shadow of Chanticleer House.*

house on a site just outside Wayne in Radnor Township. They bought ten acres of farmland in 1912 and hired the architect Charles Louis Borie to design the house, which was completed the following year. The two men had been friends and classmates at the University of Pennsylvania twenty years earlier. Borie was a partner in the then young architectural firm of Zantzinger, Borie & Medary, whose commissions later included the neoclassical headquarters of the Department of Justice in Washington, D.C.

Chanticleer House, with its stuccoed facade, mansard roof, and tall windows with recessed arches, is an elegant synthesis of French and American design. It has been changed and enlarged over the years. In 1924, when the Rosengartens decided to live in it year round, they built an addition with a new, formal dining room and a break-fast room, while the old dining room was converted into a paneled library. The swimming pool terrace was the site of a World War I victory garden that Adolph Rosengarten, Jr., remembered working as a child.

Two areas around the house were reconfigured as part of Chanticleer's transition from private home to public garden. In advance of the garden opening in 1993, a narrow bituminous path around the side of the house was laid to provide access to the rear terraces. Before he left as executive director, Chris Woods worked with landscape architect Mara Baird to replace that path with a viewing terrace that matched the elegance of the house. The resulting overlook, as it is called, functions as a place to sit and see the splendor of the gardens below, including the Serpentine and the Pond Garden. It also allows additional displays of container plantings that have come to define the landscape around Chanticleer House. The overlook's artful design and construction, not to mention the precociously large silver linden next to it, belie its age—it seems at one with the house—even as it presents a platform to view the historically recent development of the garden.

The second improvement was creating the decorative

*Gaily painted garden chairs are a hallmark of Chanticleer, and signal a view worth savoring, here the Orchard to the north of the house.*

*In late afternoon, the west facing terraces are backlit by the declining sun. The precociously gigantic silver linden stops the view.*

*The terraces of the house offer places to show off bold container plantings, to view the lower areas of Chanticleer, and, simply, to rest and take it all in.*

water feature on the patio next to the Upper Lawn, known as the reflecting pool. A classic rill or canal incorporates a rectilinear pool set on axis from an existing wall fountain. It then turns at a right angle to incorporate another wall fountain. The sound and sight of the moving water provide a sense of cool respite for visitors sitting under the shade of the patio's Asian cherry tree.

The forecourt announces the house and gives the visitor a sense of welcome, as if the walls were offering a hug. The central circle of red gravel is essential to enjoying the space; the soothing geometry and the fact it is not planted are key to opening up the space, presenting the house and inviting people to linger. It is one of the most memorable spaces at Chanticleer. There is also a restraint in the plantings, with two dominant floral elements, the ring of Japanese cherry trees and the underplantings of hydran-

*It takes careful observation to discern the ever changing raked patterns of the forecourt gravel garden, except in April when the cherry blossoms fall and accentuate the design of the moment.*

geas. The cherry trees are fleeting in their bloom, a big part of their charm, while the hydrangeas produce months of flower ornament. It's an interesting pairing.

The cherry trees are all 'Accolade', a hybrid between the magnificent, large Sargent cherry and the higan cherry. Producing clusters of clear pink, semidouble flowers, they are generally in bloom by the second week of April as the leaf buds begin to break. The petals, when they fall, land in the patterned ridges of the gravel circle. Using a homemade rake of angular metal stock, gardener Dan Benarcik creates subtle patterns in the circle. Each redrawing of the gravel takes between fifteen and forty-five minutes, depending on its complexity, and he works backward to cover his tracks. The circle is raked between two and four times a week, depending on the number of visitors. The patterns change; one day they might be concentric circles, another a basket weave, the next a parade of wavy lines.

The cherry trees flower as the massed plantings of Lenten roses hit their stride, the winter's new growth is now full, and the wine and cream nodding flowers aging but still beautiful.

The hydrangeas begin to bloom in June, on the heels of the climbing roses on the rooster pillars, a cultivar named 'Climbing Eden'. It is a vigorous hybrid opening bright pink with silver highlights, with a high petal count and a strong fragrance. It has the famous Peace ('Madame A. Meilland') rose as one of its parents. It repeats, though the August show is a shadow of June. The lovely shrub rose beneath it is Lady Elsie May ('Angelsie'), whose blooms are semidouble, coral pink, and freely produced all season long.

While the bigleaf hydrangeas flower in June and July, their mopheads and lacecaps linger as decorative elements into fall, going through endearing stages of coloration that typically wander from white to rose or blue to purple. By September the green leaves have begun their own transformation, displaying shades of red, maroon, and even orange. Hydrangeas don't fully express their blue pigmen-

*By hydrangea season in early summer, the forecourt garden leads, enticingly, to the side and rear of the house and the promise of exotic plant combinations.*

tation unless the soil has a pH below 5.0 and contains aluminum sulfate, though some varieties are inherently bluer than pink. In the neutral to slightly acidic beds at Chanticleer House, the colored hydrangeas tend to flower in pinks to mauve.

Some of the newer hydrangea varieties developed to bloom on new wood are represented here, but large, classic hydrangeas predominate, in an undelineated assortment. 'Tokyo Delight' is an extremely free-flowering lacecap, and the inflorescences have a cluster of violet flowers ringed with white rays.

'Nikko Blue' is the tried and true light blue mophead, while another Japanese hortensia, 'Otaksa', has paler blue flowerheads. Among the rarer varieties are 'Beauté Vendômoise', a six-footer with large, white, faintly blushed ray flowers, and 'Shichidanka', half the size but with lavender lacecaps with double-flowering rays. 'La Marne' is one of the latest to bloom, but patience is rewarded by a six-foot shrub with sterile flowers that are violet and green and highly indented. Light-O-Day ('Bailipse') is a lovely lacecap hydrangea with subtle leaf-margin variegation.

Amid this jumble of assorted hydrangeas ringing the forecourt, one comes to the fore in August, when the blooms of 'Preziosa' change from mauve to claret. Although a cultivar of *H. serrata,* which tend to lacecaps, its flowers are squat mopheads, somewhat like dumplings. The leaves begin to redden in the late summer.

Let's talk pots. When Chanticleer opened in 1993, the gardening world was just beginning to rediscover the exotic beauty of large-leafed tropical plants that once held sway but had fallen from favor. The introduction of novel and eye-catching varieties of cannas, elephant ears, and banana plants jump-started the craze. Dan Benarcik, who was then in charge of the Teacup Garden, took the idea and ran with it. Many of his tropical and annual plant combinations were assembled in large containers, but others were simply grown in garden beds along with hardy perennials and shrubs. He went beyond cannas, elephant ears, and bananas, though those were important ingredients, and remain so. Visitors were agog. "It was the contrast of what was so comfortable of the gardens in the Delaware Valley and the explosion coming out of it," he said. "People were delighted and Chris [Woods] said, 'More. We have to do more of this.'" Chanticleer's Teacup Garden became known far and wide as the place to go to see what was not merely a craze, as it turned out, but essentially a new horticultural art form.

So at Chanticleer House the visitor finds this form of gardening further explored with tender perennials, shrubs, annuals, bulbs, grasses, and succulents in beds, and especially in containers, including the four oversized hanging baskets of the rear facade of the house. You will find, if you are counting, more than 150 planted containers around Chanticleer House. This is an astonishing number, especially given the complexity of many of them, not to mention their fleeting seasonality. Think of the watering needs alone and the time required to nurture them.

It would be pointless to attempt to describe them all, especially since they are changed from year to year and even season to season, but talking about a few will give you a flavor of the ingenuity at play. In four slender, tapering,

*Behold the secret of effective container plantings, a bold but limited color combination with strong forms that are repeated. A spring medley of English daisy 'Galaxy Rose', 'Bull's Blood' beet, and the tulips 'Prinses Irene' and 'Paul Scherer'.*

chalky terra-cotta pots on the overlook one spring, Benarcik combined effusive plantings of a magenta pink cultivar of English daisy (*Bellis perennis*) called 'Galaxy Rose' as a filler, with a deep-purple-leafed beet green named 'Bull's Blood', above which floated the classic tulip 'Prinses Irene', which is orange-flamed magenta. Above that rose a deep purple tulip, 'Paul Scherer'. These are all strong and brooding hues, especially for the arboreal chill of April, but it is the very out-of-season passion of their color saturation and pairing that leaped at you and grabbed you by the shoulders, and demanded to know, "Have you ever seen anything like this in a pot in April?"

In mid-May, out they came, to be replaced with an entirely different combination for the warm months. The dominant plant then was *Alocasia macrorrhiza* 'Borneo Giant', an upright apple-green elephant ear that prominently displays its lower leaf venation. It was joined by a purple-leafed *Alternanthera ficoidea* 'Grenadine', a great filler for a container; a variegated phormium relative, the flax lily *Dianella tasmanica* 'Variegata'; a heat-tolerant fuchsia (most rot in the mid-Atlantic region) named 'Sanihanf'; and *Impatiens walleriana* 'Variegata'. The arrangement was rounded off with a small-leafed wire vine, *Muehlenbeckia complexa*. Each of the six plants fulfilled its own role in the ensemble, but within a considered color scheme. The green and white variegation of the impatiens, for example, echoed that of the flax lily, while its magenta flower spoke to the foliage of the alternanthera and the pendent, bicolored blossom of the fuchsia. In contrast to the spring, the cooler colors on hotter-blooded plants made for an interesting contrast.

The beds on the side of the house around the overlook terrace offer their own engaging mix of hardy and tender plants in a season-long festival that begins quietly with diminutive spring bulbs like glory-of-the-snow and ends in a blaze of leaf color and the herbaceous corpulence of such things as the towering, green-and-white striped marsh grass *Arundo donax* 'Peppermint Stick' or the Tiger Eyes

*Although Chanticleer is closed in winter, the season's snow highlights the abiding floral structure of the garden.*

gently asked Benarcik, in their own way, if he was nuts. So far, it has behaved itself.

In this same far border, the ivy 'Buttercup' spills out of an elegant terra-cotta pot—the vessel looks like a timeless olive-oil jar—and the ivy's young growth is a dazzling lemon yellow. The hue is picked up in the beautiful mounding, bamboo-leafed hakone grass. Two variegated varieties are used generously around the Croquet Lawn. The blades of 'All Gold' are solidly bright yellow. The older cultivar, 'Aureola', has the lightest yellow leaves with delicate green striping along the edges and midvein.

The balustrade between the Croquet Lawn and the house terrace contains one of the most amazing plants in all of Chanticleer, a cultivar of the American wisteria named 'Nivea'. It foliates and flowers three to four weeks after the Asian wisterias, giving the keen-eyed visitor a chance to see its lovely smooth brown bark. The April rains bestow a mahogany sheen, and it is then that you can see it has been trained playfully to encircle the balusters on its eastward journey. The blossoms appear when the vine has leafed out, making them half hidden by the foliage. They are worth studying, however; they are squat and compact,

with more substance than the Asian blooms. They remind me of a lei. The fragrance, while not overpowering, is sweet and worth pursuing.

The terrace itself is a garden of approximately thirty containers, some holding a massed planting of wild oats, with its distinctive flattened ears, others a medley of as many as ten species of hardy perennials and tender shrubs and succulents. A big house needs large hanging baskets, and the four on the main terrace have been an important element since the early 2000s, when Benarcik figured out how to fabricate the brackets to hang them from.

One year he planted an arrangement that had the *Canna* 'Thai Rainbow' growing six feet high, its ankles hidden by fluffy apple-green foxtail fern, maidenhair fern, African mallow, tall and with purple maplelike leaves, and palm-leaf begonia. The following spring, the baskets reappeared as a riot of yellow and orange ranunculus, and when their season was over Benarcik planted what were essentially trough-garden arrangements of succulents, most of them tender, some of them extravagantly fleshy, like *Echeveria* 'Perle von Nürnburg', with rosettes a gray-tinged mauve and as hefty as six inches across. There is a never a

('Bailtiger') sumac, a cutleaf shrub whose orange-red fall color has one running for a fire extinguisher.

One of the treats of spring is the flowering of the eastern ninebark, *Physocarpus opulifolius,* an underused native shrub that is highly ornamental out of bloom, with peeling bark, dark foliage even in high summer heat, and brilliant fall color. This species eventually grows very large, with arching stems as high as nine feet, though it lends itself to hard pruning. It is also adaptable to different soil conditions and is untroubled by pests and disease. Why ninebark isn't used more in place of, say, rose-of-Sharon, is a bit of a mystery. The blossoms appear in May and are white or light pink, clustered and similar in fragrance to spirea's. The cultivar Coppertina ('Mindia') has orange-red leaves that turn crimson in October. 'Diablo' is a deep purple, and Summer Wine ('Seward') is a smaller form with maroon foliage. 'Center Glow' has a yellow-orange center to its burgundy leaves, glowing like embers.

The lower lawn terrace behind the house, the Croquet Lawn, is a yearlong study in chartreuse and yellow. The beds, containers, and walls all provide opportunities to explore this theme. One of the showiest plants, in the border farthest from the house, is the eastern redbud cultivar 'Hearts of Gold', whose leaves resemble, well, hearts of gold. But they emerge red just as the tiny violet popcornlike flowers fade, clinging to the bark seemingly like no other plant in our gardens, and the leaves turn their lovely acid-green color by early May. The leaves at the branch tips, which receive the most sunlight, stay the brightest.

In each of the four corners of the Croquet Lawn garden, Benarcik planted the golden form of the smokebush, *Cotinus coggygria* Golden Spirit ('Ancot'). Three flourished, but the fourth, in the coldest corner to the far right as you have your back to the house, was caught in a deadly frost pocket. Benarcik has worked the soil here in April and found ice in it.

He wanted something with the same chartreuse foliage, and settled on the paper mulberry cultivar 'Golden Shadow'. Paper mulberry is known for two odd traits. The first is that its foliage has different forms, some deeply lobed, others entire, and the second is its ability to erupt whole new trees from its running roots. It is the ne plus ultra of exotic weed trees. Other Chanticleer gardeners

chalky terra-cotta pots on the overlook one spring, Benarcik combined effusive plantings of a magenta pink cultivar of English daisy (*Bellis perennis*) called 'Galaxy Rose' as a filler, with a deep-purple-leafed beet green named 'Bull's Blood', above which floated the classic tulip 'Prinses Irene', which is orange-flamed magenta. Above that rose a deep purple tulip, 'Paul Scherer'. These are all strong and brooding hues, especially for the arboreal chill of April, but it is the very out-of-season passion of their color saturation and pairing that leaped at you and grabbed you by the shoulders, and demanded to know, "Have you ever seen anything like this in a pot in April?"

In mid-May, out they came, to be replaced with an entirely different combination for the warm months. The dominant plant then was *Alocasia macrorrhiza* 'Borneo Giant', an upright apple-green elephant ear that prominently displays its lower leaf venation. It was joined by a purple-leafed *Alternanthera ficoidea* 'Grenadine', a great filler for a container; a variegated phormium relative, the flax lily *Dianella tasmanica* 'Variegata'; a heat-tolerant fuchsia (most rot in the mid-Atlantic region) named 'Sanihanf'; and *Impatiens walleriana* 'Variegata'. The arrangement was rounded off with a small-leafed wire vine, *Muehlenbeckia complexa*. Each of the six plants fulfilled its own role in the ensemble, but within a considered color scheme. The green and white variegation of the impatiens, for example, echoed that of the flax lily, while its magenta flower spoke to the foliage of the alternanthera and the pendent, bicolored blossom of the fuchsia. In contrast to the spring, the cooler colors on hotter-blooded plants made for an interesting contrast.

The beds on the side of the house around the overlook terrace offer their own engaging mix of hardy and tender plants in a season-long festival that begins quietly with diminutive spring bulbs like glory-of-the-snow and ends in a blaze of leaf color and the herbaceous corpulence of such things as the towering, green-and-white striped marsh grass *Arundo donax* 'Peppermint Stick' or the Tiger Eyes

*Although Chanticleer is closed in winter, the season's snow highlights the abiding floral structure of the garden.*

dull moment in this garden. It is a place where statuesque plants are used liberally, including phormiums, cycads, and agaves.

Changes in elevation add a great deal of interest to any garden, and the Upper Terrace becomes its own distinct space by way of this. One is always conscious here of the swimming pool, of the attraction of the water and the beauty of the pavilion, so the task is to acknowledge that while striving to keep the Upper Terrace a place with its own presence. Hence the long narrow border abutting the pool terrace is typically planted with taller seasonal plants that veil the pool terrace without obscuring it. As you move from the Croquet Lawn to the Upper Terrace, the border succeeds in keeping the eye fixed on the axis of the path. One year Benarcik picked a color scheme in purple-black, orange, and silver, blue, and white, the last grouping chosen to echo the swimming pool and the oxidized copper roof of the pavilion. The border contained young, upright *Eucalyptus cinerea*, the Arizona cypress cultivar 'Blue Ice', and the orange-flowered variegated *Canna* 'Tropicana'. The purple-black was provided by the red-flowered *Canna* 'Australia', the elderberry *Sambucus nigra* Black Lace ('Eva'), and a dark form of the Levant cotton plant, *Gossypium herbaceum* 'Nigra'. This idea of cool blues and brooding purples was cemented with the placement, behind the border, of a fleshy bromeliad, *Alcantarea imperialis*. Benarcik used the red form, and placed them in beautifully funereal black iron urns.

One winter Benarcik went to see the gardens and countryside of New Zealand for inspiration. "I was struck by the unifying effect of the tussock grasses, which are everywhere," he said. In the opposing beds of the upper lawn, he sought to emulate that, but in a typically imaginative color scheme of what he called tawny tans and russet browns with purple and burgundy, using unusual varieties of sedges and *Coprosma*, the latter a genus of glossy,

*To the east of the swimming pool, cordons of the apricot variety 'Harcot' bloom in early spring in an annual dodge against a late frost. The hedge is* Thuja plicata *'Atrovirens' and the grassy clumps at the base of the wall the spring foliage of* Lycoris squamigera.

evergreen tender shrubs from New Zealand and Australia. *Carex* 'Amazon Mist' is a green-leafed sedge, which was used with two red-brown varieties, the cinnamon-leafed 'Red Rooster' and the copper-bronze 'Bronzita'. Of the *Coprosma* cultivars used, 'Cutie' and 'Evening Glow' both have a bronze-green foliage. 'Evening Glow' is green with a gold variegation. It is hard to think of a plant with a shinier leaf; indeed, coprosmas make the plasticlike leaves of the Burford holly look positively dull.

In the Upper Terrace's far bed, Benarcik paired the sedges and coprosmas with eucalyptus, ninebark, *Canna* 'Tropicana', and two purple-leafed spiky plants, *Cordyline australis* 'Red Sensation' and *Phormium tenax* 'Atropurpureum'. He threw in a few sago palms for good measure.

The lawn's central patio is a stage where sculptural, upright plants are the players in a multiact drama. The productions change from year to year, and they have included displays of *Dryopteris* ferns paired with the gorgeous red-flowering swamp mallow of late summer. In one display, columns of the jasmine Fiona Sunrise (*Jasminum officinale* 'Frojas') were grown to match the golden yellow tones of the nearby smokebush, *Cotinus coggygria* Golden

Spirit ('Ancot'), coppiced each winter to produce fresh and bright stems.

The reflecting pool terrace is dominated by an old autumn-flowering higan cherry, though its name doesn't quite reflect its blooming habit in this part of the world. Shortly after leaf drop, a few buds break into pink blossom, stopping when the weather turns cold in late fall or early winter. Occasional mild spells in winter will coax more blossoms, followed by a final flush in early April as the new leaves grow.

The reflecting pool itself is given further structure and definition with the placement of four to six large containers that change from year to year. For one season, Benarcik planted handsome terra-cotta pots with the common majesty palm, softened at their base with muehlenbeckia and the 'Diamond Frost' euphorbia.

Two shrubs are worth seeking out, even out of bloom. The hybrid × *Sinocalycalycanthus raulstonii* 'Hartlage Wine', a cross between the Carolina allspice and the Chinese allspice, is planted to the right of the reflecting pool's lion's-head wall fountain. It produces maroon, roselike blooms in late spring and into summer. When Chanticleer opens its doors for the year, a daphne relative, *Edgeworthia chrysantha,* bursts into bloom near the autumn-flowering cherry. The blossoms, decorative for weeks earlier in bud, appear at the end of naked branches as conspicuous clusters of small tubelike yellow flowers with a silky white covering. The fragrance is strong and intensifies in the evening. It is as handsome in leaf as it is in bloom; its lancelike foliage, faintly tropical, is blue-green above, gray-green below.

The Sun Porch, another of Chanticleer's great memorable spaces, was built as an open, west-facing room that provided a transition between the indoors and out. It was later glazed in, no doubt making it useable for far longer during the year, especially with its lovely fireplace, but enclosing it inevitably altered its character. It became a place that was more of the house than the garden. Happily, as part of Chanticleer's public incarnation, the windows were removed and the porch was returned to the garden. It is an inviting and cosseting place, providing comforting shelter

*The reflecting pool was built after Chanticleer became a public garden, to enliven the far corner of the rear terraces.*

in the rain and cooling shade in high summer. People sit and chat here, at ease.

The windows also serve to frame views of the garden. Look through the window facing the forecourt in early April and it will be filled with a pink cloud of cherry blossoms, impossibly pretty and evocative of the whole frisson of young spring.

Within the porch, the water bowl supports whatever is blooming in season. The flowers, disembodied and framed in the blackness of the water, take on a different beauty.

The porch itself contains dozens of pots, so many that together they convey the idea of a community of house plants put out to play, made gleeful by their proximity to the great outdoors but not overwhelmed or frightened by it.

The various begonias are lovely. In one array, a three-tiered setup, a snake plant is joined by the rugose and slightly floppy begonia 'Snoopy', green with maroon specks; 'Cathedral', far more demure, with twisted little green leaves showing flashes of red-maroon from the lower leaf surface; *Begonia paleata,* a bright green, glossy-leafed begonia with a hint of pink at the heart of its circular leaves; and 'Shamus', with its contorted and twisted green leaves. There are as many as twenty begonia species or cultivars in the Sun Porch.

The planting on the mantelpiece, which is itself a garlanded monument to the carpenter's craft, has its own charm. Its floral players include a seriously curly-edged English ivy named 'Fluffy Ruffles'.

Here, you realize, at Chanticleer House, all the old barriers of lumping plants by type have broken down. This is the ultimate revelation of Chanticleer Garden.

## THE ORCHARD

The sloping field on the northeast side of Chanticleer House was once the site of the family's apple orchard. Today, the Orchard's original use is acknowledged with plant-

*The dynamic sequence of blossoms is captured in the sun porch's water container, here, an April mix of 'Ice Follies' daffodils, 'Accolade' cherry blossoms and* Puschkinia.

*All eyes are on the orchard in April. Daffodils and cherry blossoms provide the first grand display of the year.*

With the 'Actaea'
and other late season
daffodils, the rich purple-
pink blossoms of the crab
apple 'Prairifire' appear.

ings of decorative crab apples, though there are examples too of the flowering cherry 'Accolade', including a large, mature specimen at the top of the hill that is ablaze in pink blossoms in April. Spring is the main season in the Orchard, as the flowering trees shimmer above vast ribbons of spring bulbs, predominantly two "rivers" of daffodils. The gardeners put in forty thousand early- and late-season narcissus in 1991, since expanded to approximately a hundred thousand.

The display begins with sweeps of *Scilla siberica* 'Spring Beauty' and *Chionodoxa forbesii* 'Blue Giant', with the daffodil 'Ice Follies' on their heels. The *Narcissus* 'Bravoure' blooms next, and as the early-season daffodils begin to fade, others take over, including 'Salome', 'Actaea', 'Ice Wings', 'Honeybird', and 'Geranium'. These represent different forms of *Narcissus,* but many are white with creamy cups, and the idea, says the Orchard's gardener, Lisa Roper, was to select more muted varieties that would not clash with the apple blossoms.

The cherry 'Accolade', planted at both the top and bottom of the field, blooms with the early daffodils. Also at the bottom, a cluster of the yellow-flowering magnolia 'Elizabeth' blooms along with the 'Ice Follies' daffodil.

The crab apples flower later in April with the late-season bulbs, and many of the varieties are pink in bud but open white, including 'David', 'Donald Wyman', 'Jewelberry', and the Japanese flowering crab, *Malus floribunda.* The purple-red cultivar is 'Prairifire'. Crab apples have a second season of ornament, when the fruit colors up in October. The red Adirondack chairs echo the colors of the fruit. To the visitor who thinks spring is the crabs' season, the chairs seem to say, "sit awhile."

(OVERLEAF) *Once a dull field full of ailing apple trees, the Orchard has been revived with the planting of tens of thousands of daffodils and spring blossoming trees. The chairs are painted to complement the blooms of the Japanese cherry and crabapple trees.*

# CHAPTER 4

# Asian Woods

*In the lowest and remotest part of Chanticleer sits the area called Asian Woods, the distant corner where intimate trails and secluded resting spots invite quiet meditation. Here, one ambles*

or lingers in a temperate jungle that is both exotic and familiar.

Bell's Run, the stream at the edge of the estate, meanders and adds its own soft music, its far banks covered with the bold leaves of *Petasites japonicus,* through which the similarly brash bigleaf magnolia (*Magnolia*

*macrophylla*) grow taller by the year. This pairing of American tree and Asian perennial is not only aesthetically apt, with the plants' absurdly large foliage, but reflects the greater perfection of Asian Woods.

Within this one-acre garden, one finds a framework of native shade trees such as the American sycamore

*A sense of craftsmanship pervades Chanticleer, from the cultivation of plants to the design and building of the garden's singular structures. The metal bridge, by craftsman Doug Randolph, takes slender bamboo culms as its motif.*

(*Platanus occidentalis*), red maple (*Acer rubrum*), red oak (*Quercus rubra*), American beech (*Fagus grandifolia*), white ash (*Fraxinus americana*), and native persimmon (*Diospyros virginiana*). Since the area was reclaimed in the early 1990s from an overgrown and weedy woodland, the understory has developed as an enclave for East Asian bulbs, perennials, grasses, and woody plants. Think of it as a collection of choice varieties, but assembled in artistic juxtaposition.

Even if we don't know the velvet-leafed *Hydrangea aspera* or the *Sarcococca orientalis,* they are not strangers. Asian plants have been part of the fabric of the American garden for a century or more. Hostas, azaleas, bamboos, and peonies are familiar friends, and life without them, in spite of the dogma of the native plant zealots, would be unthinkable. But there is also a deeper, unconscious connection here.

Large parts of Asia share the same latitudes and continental climate as the eastern United States, but were spared

*In the autumn, a rainbow of colors captures the season and lends depth and layering to the woods.*

the ice age glaciation that diminished the plant diversity here. For close to two centuries, Western collectors have found in Japan, Korea, and provinces of China a rich source of material for display and for breeding programs.

It helps to think of Asian Woods as two gardens. Its first incarnation is as a spring garden where understory shrubs and trees and herbaceous ground covers engage in a frenetic race to put out new growth and to flower. Each is competing for light and for pollinators. The gardener's task is to match plants not just aesthetically but in such a way that no one variety elbows out its companions.

In April and May the woods are filled with jewels at every level. One has to look hard for the black and white jack-in-the-pulpit, *Arisaema sikokianum*. It's one of those plants that when you see it, you wonder how you could have missed it. The enveloping spathe is the color of the darkest chocolate, striped white, and the "jack" or spadix resembles a marshmallow in form and color. Look too for other arisaemas in spring flower: *A. tortuosum*, far taller, with a contorted spadix that grows snakelike out of the hooded spathe, and *A. consanguineum* 'The Perfect Wave', another big jack-in-the-pulpit, whose variegated spathes

*The rare maple from central China,* Acer cissifolium *ssp.* henryi. *The winged seeds or samaras, borne in showy racemes, age to a rose pink in early fall.*

are showy enough not to be hidden in the lush foliage. *A. ringens* is one of the earliest to emerge, and remains upright in leaf with the big purple flowers sheltering beneath. Peppered through the woods, visitors will find a dozen different species and cultivars of the jack-in-the-pulpit.

The woods are full of choice flowering shrubs and small trees in spring. In early April the winter hazels—*Corylopsis pauciflora* and *C. spicata*—illuminate the still open and burgeoning landscape and fill the air with their strong scent. As they fade, the azaleas and rhododendrons come into play, but in the form of subtle and sometimes dwarf varieties that are a far cry from the overblown presence of large and gaudy hybrids. The first is the deciduous Korean rhododendron (*R. mucronulatum*), bright rosy purple and the herald of the rhododendron season. Later, dwarf rhododendrons, *R. degronianum* ssp. *yakushimanum* 'Ken Janeck', from a species that originated in the southern Japanese rain forest island of Yakushima, reveal vivid trusses on demure plants. Their evergreen leaves, slender, are marked by red-brown velvety lower surfaces.

The forest floor at this time of the season is a mesmerizing place for the keen-eyed, bursting with a seemingly hesitant but unstoppable wakening of the earth. Growth spurts are discernible from day to day. As with the Solomon's seal behind Chanticleer's entrance kiosk, the curled leaf-tips of the hostas form horns, emerging from sheaths, and the subsequent loss of them to fuller foliation is almost lamented. Another earlier perennial is the epimedium, whose dainty but intricate flowers emerge with handsome, shieldlike leaves, often edged and veined in maroon, depending on variety.

Twenty-three species or varieties grow throughout the garden, from the familiar and pretty yellow-flowered *Epimedium* × *versicolor* 'Sulphureum' and the common *E.* × *rubrum,* with its red and green leaves, to far rarer epimediums that would delight any connoisseur. *E. lishihchenii*

*As spring unfurls, Asian Woods becomes a soothing study in leaf textures and shades of green. Plantings form ribbons that mimic the meandering of the stream.*

produces sprays of clear yellow blossoms above unusual matte-textured leaves. *E. grandiflorum* var. *higoense* 'Bandit' has unbelievably beautiful leaf margins, a dark purple-brown, with sprays of creamy white flowers held aloft. One of the rarest epimediums is a species from China, *E. wushanense*. It has unusually large and narrow leaflets rising to about sixteen inches, and the spidery flowers, white and butter yellow, are produced in showy clusters in early spring.

Asian Woods is home to a treasured terrestrial orchid, the Japanese lady's-slipper (*Cypripedium japonicum*), whose pouched blossom is white, but decorated with patterns of purple. The flower erupts from a corrugated, fan-like leaf. You sink to your knees to perceive it, and if others think you are in prayer, so be it. Calanthes are Japanese woodland orchids, evergreen in some climes but not here, with very different flowers than the lady's-slipper. They are arrayed on scapes, in some species sparsely and in others by the dozen. The predominant species in Asian Woods, *Calanthe tricarinata,* has showy blooms, yellow-green with ruffled maroon lips, and it blooms for three weeks from late April into May. *C.* 'Kozu Spice' is a hybrid whose flowers are red and white bicolors in spring.

If you like the familiar redvein enkianthus, you will love the specimens of *Enkianthus perulatus.* This member of the heath family forms a medium-sized shrub with white bell-like flowers that are lightly fragrant. As that towering figure of American horticulture, Donald Wyman, once lamented: "Not much grown." Three specimens bloom here in April.

By the end of May, Asian Woods takes on its different persona. Its initial nakedness gives way to flower ornament, but then the woods become a sublime place of foliage color, texture, and form. All under the parasol of the trees. It is a woodland where the temperature is palpably lower and the heat of summer is banished. The shade provides both a physical and psychological shelter. There is an abiding stillness.

No plant better suggests this shift in gear than the Japanese woodland peony (*Paeonia obovata*). It is still rare in American plant commerce, and high-priced at that. In May its single, intensely pink blossom is beautiful, but the best is yet to come. The seed pods swell through the summer until they split to reveal blue metallic seeds, presented in an open pod on what looks like red velvet.

One could not summon an Asian wood without the hosta, in all its variety. Asian Woods contains more than thirty hosta species and varieties. The woodland paths take you past classic cultivars. 'Sum & Substance' is light green, with large leaves whose venation gives a quilted effect. A single plant can mature at six feet across; it's one of the boldest leafy perennials in the woodland garden. 'Royal Standard' is another classic hosta, nonvariegated, about half the size of 'Sum & Substance' but still with great presence. It has one of the showiest blooms of any hosta and flowers white in August. The fragrance is divine. 'Krossa Regal' is another big hosta, but it stays more upright than the others, and its foliage shows a blue cast that has a subliminally cooling effect.

*The deep red umbels of* Angelica gigas *emerge in late spring.*

'Tokudama' is another standby that remains unbeatable. Its puckered, heart-shaped leaves are blue edged with light green. The leaf has so much substance that the hosta nemesis, the slug, cannot make a dent in it. Also look for 'Tokudama Aureonebulosa', which has yellow-green leaf centers edged in blue. 'Golden Button' is a yellow form, again heavily puckered.

Not all hostas are large. *Hosta venusta* is a dwarf species growing to little more than six inches. *H. tardiflora* is a giant in comparison, but still a dainty hosta that produces deep purple flowers in late October, flowering even after frost. 'Kabitan' is a sieboldii hosta with narrow, lancelike leaves that are chartreuse with ruffled green edges.

Although the main flower show is in spring, by early summer the shrub hydrangeas are in full glory. Their flowerheads will dry and add ornament for the remainder of the season. A fine assortment of other lacecap types can be found in the bed to the left of that most elegant of restrooms, disguised as a Japanese tea pavilion. These include

*Hydrangea serrata* 'Grayswood', one of the largest hydrangeas of its ilk, growing to seven feet, with lovely blue and white lacecaps that age to red-purple. *H. serrata* 'Kiyosumisawa' is a dwarf shrub whose ray flowers are white with red margins. *H. macrophylla* 'Jogasaki' is a bright pink lacecap with astonishing double ray flowers that become more intensely hued as they age.

A restroom was a given for this far corner of the garden, and one that mimicked an iconic Asian structure. The consensus was for a mock Japanese teahouse, and Thomas sent the gardener, Lisa Roper, and facilities manager Ed Hincken to Japan, primarily Kyoto, for a week to study traditional garden structures. The design was altered to lower the roof pitch and bring more crafted wood and stone into the structure. Its proportions and the careful site selection, angled at the end of curving path, allow it to retreat visually. It is a building you happen upon, but once you discover it the structure has enormous presence. It seems to reinforce the whole sensibility of Asian Woods,

*Inspired by garden buildings in Kyoto, the restroom pavilion is veiled and softened by Japanese flora.*

a place where soothing forms and lines grant an underlying tranquility to its various spaces.

Asian Woods has several of the aspera species of hydrangea that are not as well known as the macrophylla and serrata varieties. They grow into large shrubs, and some aspera forms are valued perhaps less for their flowers than for their foliage, distinguished by large heart-shaped leaves that are a rich dark green, with the texture of velvet. The stems have conspicuous hairs.

Elsewhere in the woods, the uncommon and large shrub species *Hydrangea heteromalla* blooms in June and July, with prominent white domed lacecaps.

In a garden that is all about leaf textures, one standout is a rarely used subshrub with coarse, rugose green leaves. Its foliage and habit suggest a cross between a kirengeshoma and the good old stinging nettle. Indeed, *Boehmeria spicata* is a member of the nettle family and is sometimes known as false nettle. But it invites touching, being soft and tactile and devoid of the stinging hairs of its cousin. It grows next to the path near the restroom pavilion. It dies to the ground in winter and seeds around but "controllably," said Asian Woods' gardener, Lisa Roper.

Another inhabitant of this garden worth seeking out is found on the meadow side of Asian Woods. *Syneilesis palmata* is a woodland perennial whose leaves appear in spring as a droopy umbrella, much like the native mayapples, but then it opens as a wide palmate-leafed plant that in June sends up flower stems topped with handsome clusters of small, branched flowers. The blossoms are creamy white. Roper has also planted *Syneilesis aconitifolia,* which has more finely cut leaves and flowers of a soft lavender hue. *Syneilesis* is altogether a lovely perennial and begging to be used more in gardens with shade and rich soil.

Goatsbeard is a genus that contains but two species, and both are represented here. The better known *Aruncus dioicus,* a perennial from Japan, grows to six feet in optimum cultivation. *A. aethusifolius,* native to Korea, has similar blooms but rises just twelve inches or so above the woodland floor.

Goatsbeard blossoms appear with the hydrangeas in early June and persist long enough to see their daintier doppelgängers, the astilbes, erupt into flower in late June. The tall, rose-purple *Astilbe chinensis* var. *davidii* blooms until late July, and is joined then by the lower-growing *A. chinen-*

*sis* var. *pumila,* with flower plumes of a strong violet color.

In a clearing in Bed 1, visitors will find the unexpected relief of a simple moss garden. It was once an area covered with the running ground-cover bamboo *Pleioblastus,* but the bamboo had become unruly, and trenching to contain it would have damaged tree roots, so out it came. More than anything else, the key to cultivating moss is to keep it free of fallen leaves and other tree litter—a laborious task, but the result is a space of almost sacred tranquility. A large stone has been chiseled to form a basin, a pool for floating blossoms. In the center, a sycamore tree supports an Asian species of Dutchman's pipe, *Aristolochia manshuriensis.* Its golden yellow flowers emerge just before the leaves to give a conspicuous show. A second sycamore is draped in the Chinese honeysuckle, *Lonicera tragophylla,* whose blooms are a golden yellow, showy, fragrant, and not to be missed in late May. Both vines are supported by decorative armatures of sculpted iron rebar.

The yellow wax bells, *Kirengeshoma palmata,* is one of the most attractive woodland perennials, shrublike in habit and size, with clean, large, palmate leaves that in late summer send up wiry stalks covered in conspicuous lovely yellow bell-like flowers. A large collection of toad-lilies representing twelve species and hybrids provides enchanting and exotic displays from late summer into the fall. Many are displayed in Bed 4 on the opposite side of the path from the plant list box.

Look for *Tricyrtis* 'Ama-no-gawa', white, lightly speckled dark purple; *T.* 'Kohaku', large-flowered with heavy speckling; *T.* 'Golden Gleam', golden-leafed with gray variegation, with purple flowers that emerge directly from the leaf axils; and *T. hirta* 'Miyazaki', white with faint purple speckling. *T. macranthopsis* may not be the prettiest, but it is certainly an eye-catcher. The leaves are corrugated, borne on arching stems, and the blossoms are big yellow bells that sit languidly atop the foliage.

## COLCHICUM HILLSIDE

The path out of Asian Woods to the land art feature called the Serpentine takes you along the edge of a rising meadow that seems all the more expansive after the cocooning feel

ed 'Red Garnet' mustard greens for a spring crop, followed by cotton, which flowers at this latitude but will not ripen to produce the desired filaments. Flax, with its gorgeous blue flowers that furl in the heat of the day, is in the offing.

Randolph is a no-till kind of guy, so the old crops are simply cut down and allowed to become absorbed into the soil. New crops are sown in a very narrow cultivated seed row, so that the bulk of the area remains undisturbed. By not tilling, farmers keep organic matter in the soil and carbon sequestered, and minimize soil erosion. Years of plantings here have built up the soil, and it is well on its way to becoming richly fertile, which typically takes twenty years. Thus the Serpentine, ever changing but steadily enriched, seems a fitting symbol of Chanticleer itself.

*Cotton plants bask in the steamy dawn of August. The Serpentine is an artform that exposes a post-agricultural society to forgotten but vital crops.*

# CHAPTER 5

# Pond Garden

*Open, sunny, and a glorious blend of flowers and water, the Pond Garden is the most exuberant part of Chanticleer. Imagine being in the cottage garden of a wealthy and brilliant plant maniac, throw*

in a series of cascading ponds, themselves teeming with life, and you get a sense of how special this garden has become.

The lowest and largest pond, known officially as Pond 1 but popularly as the lotus pond, is the original body of water here, a clay-lined reservoir that was (and still is) fed by a spring encased in the stone spring house. In the 1970s it was a swamp; in periods of heavy rain the stream over-

ran its banks and joined with the spring to make a sodden mess. There was never any farming in this corner of the estate. So the pond was dug to create control over this land. The spring house, which looks old but isn't, dates to this period. The five ponds above the lower pond were added later, sequentially over several years, to create a more natural effect in the landscape. The construction of the up-

*Side entrance to arbor terrace, under a rustic arch.*

per ponds then gave the gardeners the perfect setting to build plant beds around them. Their orders? Go to town. The area's gardener, Joe Henderson, fell in love with meadows after seeing the display garden Hermannshof in Germany, where a lot of North American perennials are used to great effect. "I want this wild feel," he said, "but rather controlled with color, and with shrub layers to create some structure to it."

We'll move, descriptively, clockwise from the top of the garden to the far end of the lotus pond and back again.

Chanticleer Garden is greater than the sum of its parts, but what parts! A great deal of thought has been devoted to allowing the various garden spaces, at their edges, to talk to each other. In the upper reaches of the Pond Garden, that has meant paying homage to the Gravel Garden and its use of dry-loving perennials and annuals. The hillside bed above the upper pond feature is called the Rock Ledge.

*Dazzling specimens such as this unidentified red blooming deciduous azalea present a second spring peak, flowering with alliums and Siberian iris.*

In early April, it stirs into life with a mix of naturalized spring bulbs suited for the rock garden, namely *Chionodoxa forbesii*, the grape hyacinth *Muscari azureum*, and three clusiana tulips: *T. clusiana* var. *chrysantha*, with crimson petals opening a golden yellow; 'Cynthia', a little taller with pink-red petals edged green and a purple base; and 'Lady Jane', the showiest, with pink petals opening white. The reticulated irises are among the first plants to bloom in this bed. While they are sometimes difficult to see because they are dark and live just above the soil, they are worth looking for to discover their intimate beauty. 'Harmony' is a cultivar whose upright petals, called the standard in iris-speak, are a clear light blue; the outer segments, called falls, are royal blue blotched with yellow and white. 'Marguérite' is a diminutive cultivar with dark blue petals and variegated foliage. *Iris histrioides* 'Lady Beatrix Stanley' is another small, netted blue dwarf iris for early spring, and fragrant if you are brave enough to reduce your nostrils to its level. Henderson will also add some showy Triumph tulips to extend the show, typically the classic scented 'Prinses Irene', bright orange with purple flames.

May brings another look entirely: lots of alliums and at least eight cultivars of pinks, blooming with the thyme, *Thymus serpyllum* 'Pink Chintz'. In late May the corn poppies erupt, after weeks in pendent bud. When they are ready, they raise their heads and burst into scarlet flower. They seed like mad in the fall, and when their basal rosettes form over the winter and spring they are thinned to bring a measure of control over where they flower and with whom. Poppy season is also the time for the catmints and a fabulous, intensely violet sage, *Salvia nemorosa* 'Caradonna', which is compact, bushy, and long-flowering. It is an excellent alternative to the common hybrid, 'May Night'.

By July the Rock Ledge garden reaches a pitch that continues through the year, again with obvious salutes to the Gravel Garden. The Mexican hat is having its own mariachi party, with forms in golden yellow and a deep maroon hue. In high summer this hillside is transformed into a place of herbaceous plants that demand a hot and dry site. They are subtly different from the show going on up the hill in the Gravel Garden, though echoes remain.

Above the ponds, the late spring beds on the Rock Ledge are vibrant with bulbs, annuals and perennials. The medley includes pink Silene, the pale orange Papaver atlanticum, Lupinus perennis, and the accents of the red flowering Adonis aestivum. To the left, the catmint 'Walker's Low' is paired with the orange Helianthemum 'Fire Dragon'. Behind the oxeye daisy, the deep purple Salvia nemorosa 'Caradona' has been planted with the purple allium 'Lucy Ball', the pink spikes of Gladiolus byzantinus, and the cheery, fleeting red Papaver rhoeas.

Before a magnificent stone outcropping, a lovely spring scene of the triandrus daffodil 'Hawera', grape hyacinth, and wild blue phlox.

# POND

The Spring Bed, as it is called, surrounds a fountainhead framed in stone, crafted to look natural but also not without pleasant evocations of a grotto. The water gurgling here is not from some subterranean aquifer but from a remote recirculating pump housed, ironically, in the spring house, where a real spring erupts.

The Spring Bed is in essence a transitional rock garden between the Rock Ledge and the pond gardens proper. A series of slow-growing dwarf conifers, including varieties of Hinoki false cypress, Japanese black pine, and a weeping form of the Japanese red pine, provide constancy. The herbaceous layer, by contrast, forms a continuous procession of variation and seasonal markers. In April, look for a series of essentially red species of naturalized tulips: the scarlet clumps of *Tulipa linifolia,* the orange streaked

*At season's end, as the deciduous conifers turn golden around the spring house, the pink muhly grass picks up the low sun.*

*T. whittallii,* the red, large-flowered *T. wilsoniana,* and 'Tangerine Beauty', a red and soft orange cultivar of *T. vvedenskyi.* The candy-striped 'Lady Jane' I described earlier also puts in an appearance. The tulips are followed in May by the lovely rock garden alliums, including the ground-hugging, purple-pink *Allium oreophilum* and the more spindly, purple-black *A. wallichii.* As they fade, the pinks and the corn poppies take hold and define the hill. In June, as the strangely slender and long flowers of *Kniphofia multiflora* appear, the grasses begin to assert themselves, notably the wispy tufts of Mexican feather grass, *Nassella tenuissima,* and the striking cotton candy of pink muhly grass, *Muhlenbergia capillaris.*

As you descend the hill you find three beds that form the left flank of the pond terraces. Subconsciously the visitor is drawn to the water, but the abundant flower borders are just too visually enticing and distracting.

April and May build to something wondrous, when we leave behind the hot colors of corn poppy and verbascum in the upper beds to a cooler study in blues, maroon, and chartreuse. The lady's mantle, with its water-beading foliage and acid-green flowers, brightens the edge of the beds, picking up the chrome yellows of the euphorbias. Late spring alliums join the hardy geraniums (wonderfully tall and sprawling varieties, such as 'Spinners') in furnishing blues and violets, along with the catmints and campanulas. Annual poppies of half a dozen species or more abound at Chanticleer, but it is on this side of the ponds that the largest concentration of the impossibly showy oriental poppy can be found. Here in the second half of May you will find 'Allegro', short but blowsy with scarlet flowers, along with four other outrageously flamboyant cultivars.

This is also the time of the campions, including the Maltese cross, a long-cultivated species (*Lychnis chalcedonica*) from Russia with bright red, cruciform blooms an inch across. The rose campion, *Lychnis coronaria,* is another Old

*In April, the bones of the cascading pond garden can be seen clearly. By early summer, the hillside is veiled in plant layers.*

World classic, albeit a short-lived one in the heat and humidity of the mid-Atlantic. Its scarlet flowers are borne on silvery, woolly stems.

As the verdant late spring shifts to summer, this area is graced with the most elegant and breathtaking of irises, *Iris ensata*. The Japanese iris is a big-boned iris; it's not like a tiny bulbous iris, say, and yet it has a refinement that is missing in the tall bearded iris, which is loved for other and outlandish qualities. They are both show-stoppers, but I think of the tall bearded as Ethel Merman and the Japanese iris as Audrey Hepburn. The Japanese iris is so clearly presented, so unabashedly decorative and patterned, that it seems to revel in our drooling admiration of it. And yet it is a plant that demands close study. My predecessor at the *Washington Post,* Henry Mitchell, was ostensibly a newspaperman who was paid to write prose. But it always came out as poetry. It was organic and he couldn't help it. Of the Japanese iris, which he raised from seed, he wrote, "Japanese irises are opulent beyond almost any other flower, but

they are not showy in the garden and you have to gaze at them as individuals to enjoy them." Henry had a capacity, actually a genius, for making clear what was at once so obvious—but only obvious after he had stated it. The Japanese iris is a large species, with flowers that are big but, paradoxically, not conspicuous.

In primrose season, which is in May, there is nothing more pleasant than leaning on the bridge here, looking toward Bell's Run and seeing at your feet an area bisected by the pond course to the stream known as the Primula Meadow. It is framed by lovely streamside shrubs, including summersweet and enkianthus, but the watercourse itself is directly cushioned by a field of low-growing, finely textured scouring rush. This is the field horsetail, *Equisetum arvense,* a widely distributed North American native. Shorter and finer than the common horsetail, *E. hyemale,* it is no less tenacious in moist soils. Within this mounding grasslike carpet, magenta-flowered seedlings of the Japanese primrose assert themselves. In the brook, a lone but

*The Pond Garden's upper beds in late May become a riot of red and blue-purples, with self sown poppies and hardy salvias.*

striking aquatic plant called golden club (*Orontium aquat-icum*), becomes conspicuous in early spring flower. It is a native aroid and related to the skunk cabbage, though it is the only species of its genus. The wiry inflorescence is a strong pink yielding to white, with a bright golden spadix. The other bit of the flower, the spathe, is strangely absent. Perhaps it went for a dip. The rhizomes were a source of starch for Native Americans. Another specimen is found at the top of the Pond Garden, near the bridge across the upper pond.

The walk uphill toward the spring house takes you through the Iris Meadow, which has its share of bearded iris yielding to Siberian irises and then Japanese iris culti-vars, but—belying its name—it is full of other perennials and shrubs that bring interest from April to October. In July varieties of garden phlox light up the bed in purples,

*The handmade bridge above the overflow channel of the lowest pond marks the boundary between the Pond Garden and Asian Woods. In fall, the golden foliage proves a foil to the reds of Salvia splendens 'Van Houttei' and fleeceflower 'Firetail'.*

whites, and pinks, as the black-eyed Susans begin their month of flowering. The wooded edge to the left incorporates this bed and used to contain large banks of winged euonymus. Burning bush was a favored shrub in the twentieth century for its brilliant scarlet fall color, but has proven itself an invasive exotic and has been removed here. Among the replacements is the native bramble *Rubus odoratus* (flowering raspberry), which produces lovely single violet-pink flowers in early summer. The fruit is seedy and for the birds.

The path to, and through, an area known as the meadow places the visitor in another absurdly rich explosion of flora, particularly of large grasses and perennials. The pathside clump of gooseneck loosestrife, *Lysimachia clethroides,* is a rampant spreader in moist soil, but it is an elegant plant, upright and producing its distinctive white flowers of arching racemes for weeks in summer. Again, the garden phlox enlivens the midsummer display as the switchgrasses, now fully grown, start to flower. Three stun-

ning cultivars are represented here. The classic and enduring 'Heavy Metal', with a blue cast to the foliage, is of medium width and texture. The cultivar 'Prairie Sky' has a much broader leaf and with a bluer sheen to it, similar to 'Dallas Blues' but without its propensity to flop. Rounding out these panicums is 'Cloud Nine', with markedly taller inflorescences but with narrower, gray-green blades.

The Spring House Bed offers its own garden of exploration. The spring house itself, so delightfully crafted and scaled, offers a reference point from all angles. In August, the scented, white-flowering garlic chives begins a month of bloom, drawing colorful pollinators. Near the spring house, a large and stately weeping cutleaf Japanese maple, *Acer palmatum* 'Dissectum Nigrum', pairs well with other red-purple plants, particularly the saturated hues of the tender *Salvia splendens* 'Van Houttei' in the years it is planted. The Japanese maple's leaves are deeply cut, and in spring the emerging leaves are coated with silvery hair. Its redness steps back in the heat of summer, as the warmth

*Herbaceous plants of contrasting colors and textures are combined to create vignettes throughout the garden, here,* Pennisetum alopecuroides *'Hameln' with* Musella lasiocarpa.

suppresses the anthocyanin pigments, but it goes out with a blast. The fall color is a deep, glossy red.

Several choice clematis varieties are deftly inserted in this bed, either growing on the spring house or scrambling on willing shrubs. Among the later-season varieties are two lovely viticellas, 'Purpurea Plena Elegans', with ruffled double violet-red flowers, and 'Venosa Violacea', whose petals (technically tepals) are white in the center with intensely purple margins. *Clematis potaninii* is another clematis of late summer, presenting small white flowers with golden yellow centers.

The upper ponds are marked by resident turtles and large Japanese koi. The turtles are lumbering and amusing reptiles, prone to dive if anyone gets too close. It is entertaining to watch the fish eat the algae on the turtles. There is a constant pulling in of the rear legs and the turtles seem to put up with it, but that's about all. The fish, by contrast, in their constant watery peregrinations add movement to

*When you live in an acid bog, like these sarracenias, you need to supplement your diet with insects. No one said blood-thirsty plants had to be ugly.*

the whole theater of the ponds. It is just as captivating to the oldest observer as it is to the child. The ponds hold a dozen or so varieties of hardy water lily. These include 'Charles de Meurville', whose abundant, high-petal-count lilies open a shell pink; 'Graziella', daintier in scale but hotter in color; and 'Texas Dawn', lemon-colored and fragrant. Its leaves are turned up, like pie pans, and the flowers are held a bit aloft, as with tropical lilies.

Frequent visitors to Chanticleer know that one of the most endearing aspects of the Pond Garden is that it builds season-long to a glorious peak in September. Nowhere is this better expressed than in the bed that wraps itself around the two central ponds. Asters are well represented. 'Pink Star' is a heath aster, somewhat smaller than the New England aster and smothered in tiny daisies. The New England aster 'Purple Dome', introduced by the Mt. Cuba Center, a nonprofit horticultural center near Wilmington, Delaware, has become in a few short years a valued player in the autumn garden for its compact form and sheer preponderance of vibrant purple flowers.

The blackberry lily, *Belamcanda chinensis,* is a close relative of the iris (and can suffer from the iris borer) and produces showy orange netted blooms in high summer. A few weeks later the display changes—the seed pods split to reveal clusters of shiny black seeds.

Queen Anne's lace, the wild forebear of the garden carrot, blooms here from early summer to fall, and like so many other flowering plants around the ponds it provides an important source of late-season nectar for butterflies, bees, wasps, and other pollinators. At this time, the inflorescences of the blue oat grass turn to wheat-colored seedheads. This is a small grass with a large presence. It forms a neat evergreen clump of fine, blue-gray leaves about eighteen inches high. The flowerheads are held above the mound, growing three to four feet.

One of the novelties of the late season is a weird vine, the bonnet bellflower, *Codonopsis lanceolata,* with a small purple netted flower reminiscent of the pawpaw flowers of spring. It is growing on the barberry 'Crimson Pygmy' (also known as 'Atropurpurea Nana'), whose leaves echo the interior colors of the bellflower.

The arbor is a favorite perch to view the pond terraces, or just as a place to rest in the dappled shade. Formerly a wooden structure, it was rebuilt in the winter of 2008–9.

Its pillars now consist of the same type of flecked stone used in the retaining wall behind the arbor, and they are tapered—battered, in masonry-speak—as they rise to support handsome timbers. Strong physically and visually, the beams are made of white oak. The arbor's three established wisteria vines were carefully disentangled from the old arbor and wrapped protectively while the masons and carpenters built the new arbor around them. The frigid work continued around the sleeping, bud-wrapped flowers and the vines blossomed robustly the following spring, none the worse for their ordeal. The white-flowering cultivar is the Japanese wisteria 'Shiro Noda'. The purple wisteria is also *Wisteria floribunda,* but of an unknown variety.

What looks like a huge shrub on the Rock Ledge side of the arbor is an old sycamore tree that was struck by lightning. It has sprouted freely from its stump and pro-

*A popular point of repose above the ponds, the wisteria arbor. The posts were rebuilt in stone in the winter of 2008–9.*

vides an unusual effect that no gardener on earth would be brave enough to create on purpose.

The beds in and around the arbor echo many of the plants in the Rock Ledge and the Spring Bed, including clusiana and linifolia tulips, poppies, catmint, red hot pokers, and pink muhly grass. This stunning grass, once thought more tender than it is, has a tendency to flag and fade after two or three years. It must have good drainage to stay vibrant, and burning it rather than cutting in late winter seems to help as well.

The paths from the arbor and alongside the spring house converge in a wooded corner known as the Wildflower Slope. The beds are filled with fleeting jewels of plants, especially between April and early June. Lovers of slipper orchids will want to make a beeline in the late spring, when seven species or varieties of lady's-slippers make their appearances. Look for moccasin flower, *Cypripedium acaule*, with its slipper (or, botanically, its lip) a rose pink with crimson veining. The mouthful known as *Cypripedium parviflorum* var. *pubescens* has an unusually large yellow lip. *C. reginae* is known as the showy lady's-

*The red flowering* Adonis aestivum *with the blue green foliage of* Euphorbia myrsinites, *near the Pond Garden arbor.*

slipper for its gorgeous flower, with creamy white upper petals above a bulbous lip that is blushed and then marked magenta. Whoever named it got it right: it is the queen of native lady's-slippers.

*Trillium catesbaei* is a white and pink nodding trillium that is widely distributed in the southern Appalachian Mountains, often found, as it is here, in a dry woodland setting amid stands of rhododendron and mountain laurel. It is slower to spread from seed than the white trillium, which is represented here in the double form, *T. grandiflorum* 'Flore Pleno'. A species named Underwood's trillium is native to eastern Alabama, and it produces wine-colored flowers held at the center of the prettiest leaves, silvery green along the midvein and then mottled in several shades of darker green. Vasey's trillium is another nodding species, but tall and with conspicuously veined flowers that are maroon. The yellow-flowered trillium is the popular *T. luteum.* The Pond Garden, dramatic in its vistas, its necklace of animated ponds and its floral exuberance, is Chanticleer at its brassiest. The quiet flowering of the trilliums provides a calm before the storm.

Thelypteris noveboracensis *with* Phlox divaricata *'Sherwood Purple'.*

# CHAPTER 6

# Stream Garden

*In April and May, when spring blossoms paired with the symbolic fertility of the rushing stream capture the sudden and unstoppable burgeoning of the season, Chanticleer's Stream Garden comes into its own.*

The first showy color comes in the form of broad drifts of the daffodil 'Ice Follies', whose lines follow the meandering path of the stream. Look closely and you will see another streamside beauty, the native bellworts, *Uvularia grandiflora,* with lemon-yellow petals held like clusters of dangling pennants.

The blue-flowering quamash is the defining spring plant for the Stream Garden. The tops of the stream banks are planted with thousands of specimens of this native spring bulb, which was historically an important source of food for many Native American tribes. The species most often used for food is *Camassia quamash,* noted by

*Beware the spouting toad.*

Lewis and Clark in 1805 on their expedition westward; they found its bulb to be onionlike "and sweet to the taste."

Native American women would laboriously dig up the bulbs with sticks and roast them slowly in a fire pit for days, making a cake of them. In the Stream Garden at Chanticleer the camassias are planted generously and left to multiply, which they will do in moist conditions (and decidedly peter out in dry soil). *Camassia scilloides* is native to the eastern United States and has shorter petals than the true quamash. But the camassia planting here is of 'Blue Danube', a cultivar of the West Coast *C. leichtlinii* with deep indigo-blue blooms, a cluster of stars redolent of the related hyacinth. The length and beauty of the camassia show is dependent on a cool, even spring. A few days of a precocious 80 degrees or more can blast them away for the year.

The Japanese primroses flower at the same time and provide a different experience of the stream bed in April and May. Happy in this moist environment, they seed freely and spread with great seedling variation.

The water wheel  was installed in the 1940s to pump water to the fountains of the main house and now func-

tions as a piece of kinetic art. It is set in a bed of ostrich fern, whose emerging, coiled croziers are mimicked in the black railing of the iron fence, which was made by the gardener of the Stream Garden, Przemek Walczak. Ten varieties of clematis grow here, finding the open and airy railings a perfect means of support. 'Lagoon' produces nodding, bell-like flowers in early May; a violet-blue 'Jadwiga Teresa', also known as 'Général Sikorski', is a large-flowered midseason clematis with six broad, overlapping tepals of deep blue. 'Olgae' is another nodding bell-like clematis, but it flowers later than 'Lagoon' and is fragrant. 'Silver Moon' is an early large-flowered cultivar, one of the rare silver-mauve clematis. It was bred by Percy Picton, an undergardener at Gravetye Manor to the father of modern horticulture, William Robinson. A Robinson introduction is also grown here, 'Gravetye Beauty', a red-flowering hybrid of *Clematis texensis.*

The circular pond on the north side of the Stream Garden enjoys its own whimsy. The toad sculpture spits water at people, the younger the better. If you look into the murky well of the pond you see a bronze statue of a maiden, inhabiting a translucent underworld. The statue once adorned the formal garden of Minder House and had been placed in storage. One day, when Chris Woods was away, Walczak lowered the statue into the pond. When Woods returned, "he loved the idea," said Walczak. She has been there since, keeping company with the native rosy red minnows and a large catfish.

The eastward side of the Stream Garden will lead to the native woodland under development, and it is already planted with rare and choice indigenous trees and shrubs, along with perennials and ferns.

In its simplicity and openness, the Stream Garden is one of the most charming and relaxing areas of Chanticleer. It is a garden one can both move through and rest within. The movement of the water wheel and the relentless coursing of the stream bestow a pulse, a calm vitality to the space.

(OVERLEAF) *A decorative path offers a sidetrack into the woods.*

# CHAPTER 7

# Minder Woods, the Ruin, and Gravel Garden

*There are three woodlands within the thirty-five acres of Chanticleer Garden. Each is quite different in character. The three-acre native woodland, still under development, will mature in the*

decades to come and define the stream valley at the northern fringe of Chanticleer. Within its framework of American beech, white oaks, tulip poplars, and sycamores, visitors will find all that you might expect in a mid-Atlantic forest, but in artful arrangement. Spring bulbs, spring ephemerals, ferns, and perennials will cover the ground, yielding to the successive flowering of understory shrubs, trees, and vines. Autumn brings its own mantle of leaf

*By August, the foliage and venation of the hardy begonia is agreeably conspicuous. The stems of a* Pieris japonica *have been shaped to reveal a pleasing form.*

color, which we tend to take for granted in the temperate deciduous woods of the eastern United States, but which is precious and deserves veneration.

The second sylvan pocket, the one-acre Asian Woods (explored in chapter 4), is a celebration of the bounty of Asian flora and its sublime adaptation to the American garden.

The third shade garden is Minder Woods. Pronounced Minn-der, it was named by a former owner of this part of the estate. Chanticleer's creator, Adolph Rosengarten, Jr., lived in nearby Minder House, now the location of the Ruin.

All three of these woods perform a vital role in the enjoyment and understanding of Chanticleer. They provide physical respite as you tour the garden, a place to sit in the shade, but they offer too an opportunity to rest the mind. The floral nature of shade gardens reduces the sensory pitch in a way that is soothing and meditative,

*Rustic paths move through a woodland floor covered with ferns and perennials.*

and the reduction in light and temperature has its own cosseting effect.

## MINDER WOODS

At just over two-thirds of an acre, Minder Woods differs from the other woodlands in two essential ways. First, it is at the center of the garden, and is the hub from which all else radiates. The other woodlands, by contrast, are enjoyed on the fringes. Second, it is more traditional in the sense that it doesn't exclude flora for a theme, which an Asian or native woods must do. Rather, it brings together plants for their companionship and beauty alone.

But don't confuse eclectic with chaotic. This is very much a considered garden, with orchestrated movements through the year and plant groupings and combinations borne of knowledge and experience. It is given much of its structure by an ancient and towering red oak, sweetgum trees, hemlocks, white pines, and firs.

Minder Woods is a place that whispers in April, when many of the herbaceous plants have yet to arrive fully and the deciduous canopy is still filling out. No plant personifies this wondrous stirring better than the evergreen shrub *Pieris japonica*. Its clusters of white, bell-like flowers, its ericaceous racemes, pronounce it a proud member of the heath family. The blooms fall like fountains at the start of the season. In this sublime moment, balanced between the cold of winter and the heat of summer, the new leaf rosettes of the pieris emerge an intense red. In some varieties they are as decorative as any flower and, like a rainbow, are made all the more precious by their transience. Warmth chases away most of the red pigmentation, and when it leaves, pieris lovers yearn for the next spring.

Where the woodland path opens on the Ruin side, species pieris form a towering arch. Closer to the path's central bench, the similarly tall and open *Pieris japonica* 'Dorothy Wyckoff' (the books call it "compact," but their authors obviously don't have in mind an old shrub in the woods) displays maroon flower buds that open pink fading to white. The fresh leaf rosettes are of the brightest scarlet, glowing above the clenched silver-green shepherd crooks or croziers of the ostrich fern.

*P. japonica* 'Temple Bells', found in the same bed, is smothered in white panicles in spring, and the new growth is a purple-bronze color, sometimes apricot. The cultivar 'Valley Valentine' is marked by its fragrant pink flowers, which in bud are an intense rose-pink, capped with white calyces.

The flowering quince, *Chaenomeles speciosa,* is another cheerful harbinger of spring, its waxy flowers appearing on bare stems, and it is found in the large, sweeping bed that extends from the southeast entrance to Minder Woods all the way down to the embankment below the Gravel Garden's wisteria arbor, known as the Winter Shrub Border. The quince is presented in two distinct plantings, one at the uppermost part of the Winter Shrub Border, the other closer to the arbor above.

The aptly named 'Apple Blossom' cultivar looks like its namesake, with white single blooms blushed pink, but they appear a month earlier than the real McCoy and are

*The start of the season is marked by spring bulbs and old pieris shrubs draped in their creamy white racemes.*

far more persistent. 'Marmorata' is a white and pink bi-color. Flowering quinces are an essentially old-fashioned garden shrub and were favored at a time when gardeners were content to let sprawling woody plants do their thing for two or three weeks a year and then retreat into the landscape. We now want trees and shrubs to have more than one season of ornament, and to be smaller in scale. That said, however, the big-boned, twiggy, spiny flowering quince is still a beloved herald of the season for its brassy, frost-defiant blossoms.

'Snow' is a clear white cultivar of *Chaenomeles speciosa.* The bed also contains a hybrid of *C.* × *superba,* 'Crimson and Gold', a fantastic plant, lower and more spreading than the other varieties and with a large, two-inch blossom that is clear and matte red with golden anthers. The true fruiting quince is another plant entirely, a pear relative named *Cydonia oblonga,* though the fruits of *Chaenomeles* can be used for preserves and they are blessedly free of the pests and diseases that afflict apples and members of the *Prunus* gang, including peaches and cherries.

At this time, the woodland floor is stirring with such beauties as the early, violet-blue *Crocus tommasinianus*

and *Cyclamen coum,* and later in April the blue-flowered *Brunnera* and Virginia bluebells. A mophead form of the Chinese snowball viburnum (*V. macrocephalum* f. *macro-cephalum*) is a showy player at this time; the inflorescences emerge an apple green, becoming white in May.

Mature and dazzling specimens of the buttercup winterhazel are found in the heart of the woods, as well as the Winter Shrub Border. The latter is also alive in early season with the common but never vulgar daffodil 'Ice Follies', a large cupped narcissus, white with a frilled yellow corona. On the Ruin side of the woods, gardener Laurel Voran plants tulip hybrids that change from year to year but might include the lily-flowering 'Maytime', red-violet with white edges, 'Marilyn', white with violet flames, and 'Moonshine', a golden yellow.

Perennial spring bloomers include Virginia bluebells, windflowers, and grape hyacinths. The spring snowflake, often mistaken for a large, tardy snowdrop, is not to be missed. The white petals have tiny green heart-shaped markings just below the apex.

The southern entrance to the woods is marked by two sentinel plants, to the left the large shrub magnolia, *M.*

*sieboldii,* and to the right the Japanese cherry 'Snowgoose'. The magnolia is festooned with fragrant nodding flowers in spring, lasting for weeks. The tepals are considered the purest white of any magnolia and encase highly decorative, rose-colored anthers. The earlier flowering cherry, similarly, has the whitest of blossoms.

April and May signal the showy appearance of rhododendrons. More than a dozen species and cultivated varieties are represented in the beds on either side of the central path. They number several native species as well as cultivars with Asian blood in them.

Several azaleas are part of the rhododendron mix. The pinxterbloom azalea, *Rhododendron periclymenoides,* gets its common name from the old Dutch word for Whitsuntide or Pentecost, *Pinxter.* This native deciduous azalea blooms invariably before Pentecost (the seventh Sunday after Easter), perhaps providing another indication that the spring blooming cycle has advanced over the past two centuries. The pastel pink blossoms appear as the shrub begins to leaf out, and they are showy, particularly because of the curving stamens that extend way beyond the throat of the blossom. Pinxterblooms are quite fragrant and have

been used by hybridizers to inject a measure of fragrance to their crosses. A second deciduous native azalea, the pinkshell azalea (*R. vaseyi*), has similar bloom color, though the flowers are not quite as exquisite or perfumed as the pinxterbloom's. Gertrude Jekyll was fond of it.

Another prominent azalea, descended from the Asian *R. mucronatum,* is nonetheless quite at home here, both in its name—'Delaware Valley White'—and as one of the classic varieties of the mid-Atlantic region, bred for its winter hardiness and distinct and profuse white blossoms.

The Asian species of rhododendron, *R. decorum,* is a large shrub native to the highlands of the Yunnan province of China, with trusses that are white to soft pink. Another big rhododendron, but a native species, *R. maximum,* was valued by the earliest settlers to America, who knew it as the Great Laurel. In the 1730s the Philadelphia nurseryman John Bartram collected specimens and seeds in the upper Schuylkill River valley, not too far from where Chanticleer stands today, and sent them to eager recipients in England. They were displayed for their own majestic and novel beauty in the finest country properties. Eventually they were used to create the vast number of rhododendron hybrids that gripped British gardeners in the nineteenth century. The same role awaited another East Coast native, *R. catawbiense,* represented in Minder Woods by the lilac-purple species and its classic varietal offspring, 'Roseum Elegans', with lavender flowers, globular trusses, and deep lustrous green leaves.

The spring woods are brightened by smaller hybrids as well, such as *R.* 'Windbeam', whose blossoms are white, tinged pink. *R.* 'Mary Fleming' grows to just four feet, with uncharacteristically small leaves and lovely funnel-shaped flowers that are cream with a rose blush.

June signals hydrangea season, which brings a frisson of sorts amid the quiet merriment of dappled shade and foliar juxtaposition. Bed 24, which is to the left of and behind the central bench, is particularly rich in summer hydrangeas. It includes the species *Hydrangea aspera,* typically less showy in flower but gorgeous in gigantic leaf, here represented by the cultivar 'Mauvette', which is the exception to the rule. It has diminutive leaves and brassy lacecaps, and the purple fertile florets are surrounded by a ring of sterile flowers—often called rays or ray florets. More familiar is the bigleaf lacecap, *H. macrophylla* 'Blue Wave', which grows to six feet and whose blossoms are blue and encircled with light pink rays.

Fans of mopheads, also known as hortensia hydrangeas, will enjoy the *H. macrophylla* 'Forever Pink', a small, four-foot hortensia with perfect round flowerheads, a rich pinky blue. Hortensias have blooms that consist of rounded clusters of all large and sterile flowers. These are the most showy of the hydrangeas. Lacecaps, in contrast, consist of a ring of conspicuous sterile flowers surrounding an inner cluster of tiny fertile flowers, where seeds then develop.

Two of the most beautiful lacecaps inhabit this area, namely *H. serrata* 'Blue Billow', remarkable for its intense, iridescent blue fertile flowers and white rays, and 'Tokyo Delight', which is the ultimate classic blue-flowered, white-rayed lacecap, as delightful as any in its broad habit and prolific flowering. 'Preziosa' is a serrata cultivar with small rounded mopheads variously white or blush, aging to burgundy. This cultivar is cherished in southeastern Pennsylvania as a reliable bloomer. There are four unidentified macrophyllas by the path, late-season blue-flowering hydrangeas.

At this time, the flowering quince bed below the wall (the quince now willing to show immature fruit but little else) is rendered magnificent by another showy shrub, the bottlebrush buckeye, *Aesculus parviflora*. Its bottlebrushes are discernible in May as white shoelaces, slender, wiry, and held miraculously aloft. The florets open from the bottom up in late June, giving several weeks of display. This is a large native shrub, reaching eight to ten feet tall and as much as fifteen feet or more across. "Not a shrub for the small garden," sniffs the late, great Donald Wyman in his gardening encyclopedia. Fortunately, the bed that descends to below the wisteria arbor of the Gravel Garden, known as the Winter Shrub Border, is anything but constricted. In summer, the bed is also alive with robust perennials, including kniphofias, Russian sage, liatris, lilies, and finally the asters. *Aster laevis* 'Bluebird' is a robust and free-flowering aster, more vase-shaped than mounding and full of large clear blue flowers. *A. ptarmicoides*, sometimes lumped as a goldenrod, is shorter and topped with clus-

*Herbaceous and woody plants form a mesmerizing tapestry at season's end.*

ters of showy white, yellow-centered daisies. 'Annabelle', the showy white native smooth hydrangea, does its thing between July and September, when the inflorescences go through their perfect color sequences of white to green to rose.

Back in the heart of Minder Woods, the ferns look as fresh as they did in May. Ostrich ferns, as big as temperate ferns get, border the path and just look junglelike, lush and magnificent. This native bog fern has spread in fully half the beds of Minder Woods. The lovely, hardy maidenhair fern, *Adiantum pedatum,* dances with the Virginia bluebells in late April but by June is a lovely foil for the impressively large stand of yellow wax bells, *Kirengeshoma palmata,* then pushing up black flower stems above the palmate foliage. It's a big-leafed perennial that thinks it's a shrub.

By midsummer the hardy begonias are already showy, their leaves arrayed in horizontal planes and the venation beneath forming a red structure against the brown-green leaf tissue. They will change in the weeks ahead, but carry ornament through to October.

In August and September they burst into flower, producing arching stems laden with soft satiny pink blooms. The petite blossoms resemble paper darts, more so when they form their seed pods in early autumn. The pods grow heavier with ripening seed, and the stems bend more to reveal coral pink coloration.

In September and October the importance of leaf texture comes to the fore, and the layering of ground covers, shrubs, and understory trees. The lacecap hydrangeas, now rose-colored, provide an agreeably big leaf form, and the variegated bamboo or dwarf white-stripe, *Pleioblastus variegatus,* engages in a playful dance with the shifting dappled shade. Laurel Voran, the gardener, has the bamboo in her crosshairs, however. "Too invasive," she says.

Many woodland beauties are keen to bloom in spring, perhaps when their flowers are more conspicuous to pollinators, or to allow a long season of seed set. In addition to the yellow wax bells and hardy begonia, however, two other Asian perennials reveal the virtues of patience, of waiting until the spring flurry is but a memory before flower-

*In early fall, mature sourwood trees come to the fore with their stunning wine-colored leaves.*

ing. The Japanese anemone cultivar 'Andrea Atkinson' has gorgeous single white flowers with orange centers, and it blooms for weeks. *Tricyrtis hirta* 'Miyazaki' is a cultivar of the toad lily whose pendent stems are stuffed at every axil with exotic flowers reminiscent of orchids, astral blossoms a pale lavender speckled with purple spots. There is an orchidlike exoticism to them. The toad lilies are planted prominently on either side of the path as it winds to its southern entrance.

There are other late-season moments for the keen observer. One of the weirder plants in Chanticleer is the white baneberry, *Actaea pachypoda,* a native perennial that in late summer forms showy clusters of berries that are a porcelain white with a dark spot. They radiate from magenta stalks. Its other common name, doll's eyes, suggests something amusingly macabre. But only for a moment. In autumn Minder Woods takes on an air of transcending serenity. The crickets are chirping merrily but you can still, literally, hear a leaf drop. It is a gentle reminder that the season draws to its close. One tree insists on going out with a bang, to our delight. The woods contain four mature specimens of the sourwood, *Oxydendrum arboreum,* whose drooping flower panicles of summer progress to showy seedpods, countless strands of pearls draped against a layered foliage, now an intense wine red.

## THE RUIN

The idea of something in ruin being attractive seems counterintuitive, but even the casual observer realizes that there is something truly artful, creative, and yes, endearing, about this oddity.

Approach the Ruin from the hillside path on the opposite side to Minder Woods, where you can see its silhouette at the top of the hill, and you will proceed through it in the way the designers wanted. The rooms become pro-

*Weeping Norway spruces are framed from within the Ruin, like ghosts wandering aimlessly, and amiably, around the place.*

*Scattered about the Ruin's "library" are books by sculptor Marcia Donahue. What do books and gardens share? Leaves, of course.*

gressively, if subtly, more decayed from front to back and right to left and should be enjoyed in sequence.

Before entering, though, observe the seven weeping Norway spruces (*Picea abies* 'Pendula') and the lone weeping silver fir (*Abies alba* 'Pendula') that haunt the hillside approach to the Ruin. Somber-looking plants to begin with, they take on a human quality in the context of the Ruin, perhaps calling to mind amiable ghosts, their heads bent in a state of constant bewilderment. Two more of the spruces haunt the Ruin itself.

The Ruin sits on the footprint of the home of Adolph Rosengarten, Jr. It was the brainchild of Chris Woods, Chanticleer's first executive director. In Woods's native Britain, the majestic ruins of places such as the gothic Tintern Abbey in South Wales or the Rievaulx Abbey in Yorkshire, with roofless walls and ornate stonework that evoke a wondrous sense of past, are a brooding presence in the landscape and, yes, beautiful. That eighteenth-century arbiter of garden design, Horace Walpole, commended the decayed classical villa of the Emperor Hadrian for inspiration, "the ruins and vestiges of which still excite our astonishment and curiosity."

Chris Woods cautioned against reading too much into the folly at Chanticleer, except to say that it was open to the various interpretations of each visitor. But there is an undeniable whimsy about it, from the way the leaded glass window of the plant list box has a faux broken pane to the titles of the books in the "library." One is titled "Moss," another "Fossils," and another "Erosion." More than two dozen stone books and other pieces by sculptor Marcia Donahue litter the Ruin's library, carved from sandstone, green marble, and schist.

Woods had visited Donahue's garden in Berkeley, California, about a decade before the Ruin project and remembered her sculptures for their beauty and playfulness. He later brought the Chanticleer board of trustees to the West Coast to see her work. In addition to the books, Donahue carved the acorns at the Ruin's entrance, the faces in the fountain, the face boulder in the Sporobolus Hillside below the Ruin, and the ceramic bamboo at the rear of Chanticleer House.

Composed of a gray schist flecked with mica, the Ruin has darkened somewhat since it opened in 2000. In a spring drizzle, the stone turns charcoal gray and glistens.

Minder House was built in 1925 as a typically handsome, pre–Depression era Main Line abode, a solid stone farmhouse, supremely elegant but without pretension. Rosengarten loved its coziness and lived there from his marriage to Janet Newlin in 1933 until his death in 1990. Widowed in 1982, he married Virginia S. Denison in 1986; she remained in Minder House until 1997, and she died in 2001.

The initial idea was to create the ruin by partially dismantling the existing house, but that was deemed unsafe and unsightly. The old house was demolished and the Ruin built on its foundations after the basement was filled in.

Both the dining room and library mimic the functions of the original house. The dining room is dominated by a stone table that doubles as a reflecting pool. A thin sheen of water extends to the edges from a central canal about six inches deep.

To those who see an underlying dark humor to the whole Chanticleer Ruin experience—and many do—the table of black, polished granite suggests a sarcophagus. Chris Woods once remarked that he saw the ruin as "darkly more theatrical" than initially conceived, and if there were a banquet at this table, it would not be a merry affair—rather, as he once told me, more like "a Thanksgiving table where the family isn't getting on too well."

The water table is scaled to dominate the room without overpowering it, and the design has a conscious restraint to it. "Chris and I didn't want it overwrought," said Mara Baird, the project's landscape architect. It was inspired by sybaritic banquet tables in the Italian Renaissance, in which guests received their victuals on floating plates. It sits on a "rug" whose scrolls were fashioned from roof tiles salvaged from the old house.

A ruin suggests abandonment. By humans, yes, but not by plants. A neglected landscape is soon reclaimed by the plant kingdom. Evoking that chaotic floral invasion in what is actually a highly controlled garden is part of the underlying playfulness. It begins at the entrance, where two carved acorns by Donahue, along with a tablet showing a fossilized oak leaf, are the symbolic seed for real white oak seedlings growing around them.

Inside the dining room, to your left near the fountains, look for the paulownia tree growing from inside and out the window. This is a classic weed tree that would take advantage of the situation, although if left to its own devices it would have preferred to grow straight up rather than through the window, a detour that is very much the gardener's art.

The mantelpiece plantings in the dining room consist of another mix of hardy and tender plants, mostly succulents. Typically the mix will include the distinctive deep purple rosettes of the tender *Aeonium arboreum* 'Zwartkop' (repeated in the library), the hardy white-flowered stonecrop *Sedum ternatum,* the strawberry geranium or *Saxifraga stolonifera,* and, fittingly here, the ghost plant or *Graptopetalum paraguayense.* The last is a gorgeous fleshy succulent, native to Mexico, with large silver-blue leaves tinged pink.

Look for trailing plants in soil pockets in the walls in the Ruin; these have included a spindly, silver-leafed *Arc-*

*The scroll work on the "rug" is made of tiles recycled from the house razed to build the Ruin. The table to the left is dark but mirrored by a shallow reflecting pool in its surface.*

*totis* of unknown species, a hardy spurge named *Euphorbia myrsinites,* and a swallowwort from Madagascar, *Cynanchum compactum,* with leaves reduced to scales and fleshy beanlike stems that grow to about twenty inches. A similar plant, but with thinner stems, is *Rhipsalis clavata,* growing in the Ruin's outside wall pockets. "I can't resist weird, succulent-y things," said Laurel Voran.

As you make your way to the flooded room, you hear the sound of water gushing from one basin to the next, coursing along three chutes and two sheeting walls. Here, Donahue carved six faces or masks, one on the wall, one in the corner, three floating above the water, and one, oh dear, sinking. Or is it emerging from the depths?

"When I carved the faces," she said, "I wanted them to have the expression I would imagine a rock to have. I like to have it very solid and meditative and settled. They're not anxious, they're just sitting there, and it's OK."

The house begins to break down at this point; the pillars have lost their stone cladding and are now wooden posts. They hold chain-linked iron buckets, built to move coal from one floor to another in a downtown Philadelphia church that was demolished in the 1990s. They now contain burro's tail (*Sedum morganianum*) and other succulents.

The plantings in the Ruin are chosen not for their floral display but for the beauty of their foliage, form, and texture, although tulips, often in white, grace the early season, followed by poppies that have seeded themselves, including the soft orange Spanish poppy, *Papaver rupifragum,* and *P. triniifolium,* another muted orange biennial poppy, native to Armenia.

Ivies have fallen from grace in the United States because of the invasive nature of English ivy, *Hedera helix.* This is only a problem when the vine reaches its pinnacle and changes to a mature fruiting form, producing seeds that are dispersed by birds. The Ruin holds several really interesting and worthy cultivars. In the bed to the right of the acorn entrance, the gardeners have planted *Hedera nepalensis* 'Marbled Dragon', angular, dark green, with conspicuous venation that fades as the season progresses. In the

*Planters and other niches hold lavish arrangements of tender succulents.*

bed behind the flooded room, you will find the odd *H. helix* 'Medusa', stiffly upright and with five or more forward-pointing lobes instead of the classic three-lobed ivy leaf, and more rounded. On the wall of the fountain the gardener has trained the big-leafed Persian ivy cultivar 'Sulphur Heart', with lovely golden variation to the leaf center.

Moving to the library, the stand of upright evergreens is the Japanese holly cultivar 'Sky Pencil', little soldiers marching in a bed of Irish moss, *Sagina subulata.* In island beds in and near the library and against the dining room wall, the Chinese maple species *Acer davidii* shows off its bark, green with white striations. It belongs to a group of acers called snakebark maples for the reptilian trunk markings. Again, the ground covers are subdued displays of shades of green and contrasting textures.

In the library's lower fireplace, a Japanese painted fern dances like the flames from a beech log. Regard the second-floor fireplace above it, now framed by the ever-ascending climbing hydrangea. Its vine tips flicker like flames around the fireplace in some sort of cosmic symbolism.

In a small pocket bed just outside the library, you will find a couple of moisture-loving rushes: the scouring rush, *Equisetum hyemale* var. *robustum,* and the bulrush, *Schoenoplectus tabernaemontani* 'Albescens'.

The broken pot outside the Ruin announces the ironic peak of decline. The bed is alive with flowering bulbs and perennials, in contrast to the subdued palette within the Ruin, and this floral display not only suggests an encroaching meadow but sets the stage for the Gravel Garden.

By late spring, the bed is ablaze the white blossoms of the low-growing Greek yarrow, *Achillea ageratifolia,* the blossoms of the purple-leafed cranesbill, *Geranium maculatum* 'Espresso', and the lovely white-flowered, blue-stemmed pink, *Dianthus* 'Mendlesham Maid'.

The bed is full of long-flowering summer perennials, all of them charming but none more so than the Mexican hat, *Ratibida columnifera,* an aster relative producing dozens of quirky, sombrero-like flowers. Other summer bloomers include *Agastache* hybrids and the unusual green-flowered milkweed, *Asclepias viridis.*

*Beyond the polished granite water table, a squad of 'Sky Pencil' Japanese hollies witnesses the progressive phony decay.*

Doug Randolph, Chanticleer's craftsman, picked up the whimsy of the Ruin in creating the sofa and chairs of stone under the shade of magnificent specimens of tulip poplar, red oak, and basswood trees. The furniture is assembled from the same vernacular mica schist as the Ruin, though the "cushions" are of Pennsylvanian black granite, which arrived in a monolithic slab six feet wide and twelve feet long. They are surprisingly comfortable. The "remote control" is a wry touch, and if you look carefully you can see a rising sun radiating to its buttons. "Sundial," says Randolph. The backs of the furniture are clad in climbing hydrangea.

At the feet of this furniture is a living carpet of low-growing plants, whose threads include variegated liriope, mondo grass, the bugleweed cultivar 'Valfredda', Japanese sweet flag (*Acorus gramineus* 'Pusillus'), and various fescues.

*Completing the pantomime of the Ruin, a sofa and chair are cast out, not to the curbside but around a rug of low-growing ground covers.*

## GRAVEL GARDEN

One of the most open, sunny, and—thanks to a great deal of soil amendment—free-draining areas of Chanticleer is the Gravel Garden. Essentially it is a rock garden of low-growing herbaceous plants, but it contains as well a considerable array of trough gardens. It is a garden you walk through, not around, and this brings you close to diminutive plants that deserve a keen viewing. The broad stone steps take you down a series of seventeen levels to the wisteria arbor, and then to the right to a side garden with stone benches. In the Rosengartens' day it was a place of rose gardens and formal terraces, but has since entirely changed in character and horticultural complexity.

The Gravel Garden stirs in April, but quietly, with miniature daffodils and species tulips yielding to columbines. One feels that the weeks of spring are merely a pre-

lude for a garden that hits its stride in early summer and then remains beautiful and interesting well into the fall.

Although it is an herbaceous garden, it is given structure by the repeated use of certain plants. They guide and stop the eye and bring echoes of themselves like a recurring motif in a musical composition. Grasses play a major role in this effect, particularly the upright *Calamagrostis* × *acutiflora* 'Karl Foerster' peppered throughout the terraces. It is paired in the uppermost bed with side oats grass, *Bouteloua curtipendula,* shorter and different in habit than the calamagrostis, with pendent oatlike seedheads bearing tiny reddish flags in summer.

The wispy Mexican feather grass, *Nassella tenuissima,* is found throughout the terrace beds, repeating its mound of fine-textured blades. Butterfly weed (*Asclepias tuberosa*) and asters are also repeated in considered fashion.

Some of the showiest grasses are found in or near the arbor beds close to the grass circle terrace, represented by

*The wisteria arbor supports a number of magnificent woody vines, but also functions to frame and enclose the expansive Gravel Garden.*

three quite different selections of switchgrass. 'Rotbraun', as its German name suggests, has thick blades tinged a ruddy brown. 'Northwind' is the most upright of the panicums, with thick bluish blades and the capacity to stand tall in a tempest without flopping. Unfortunately, the same can't be said for the third switchgrass cultivar, 'Dallas Blues', a gorgeous ornamental grass that has a tendency to splay in late summer. When it behaves, its violet flowerheads hover about seven feet high, crowning steel-blue foliage.

The nearby ornamental urn measures forty-two inches across, and in frost season it is wrapped in a tarp and sits on a wooden pallet to keep its base dry. Cold alone is not the enemy of terra-cotta in winter; it is the combination of moisture and freezing that destroys clay pots.

In May the thymes begin to bloom alongside the pinks and poppies. Thyme is one of the signature plants of the Gravel Garden. Fifteen species and another fifteen named varieties are planted in nine beds and alongside the ten highest steps.

The first weeks of summer provide a golden moment, with the upper beds planted with a mixture of Tennessee coneflower, purple coneflower, and wild quinine, *Parthenium integrifolium,* with its umbels of white flowers. The inflorescences of the calamagrostis, still young in July, are a deep russet color, and the *Asclepias tuberosa* has begun its long season of orange bloom. The last is paired daringly at the bottom of the garden with the purple poppy mallow, *Callirhoe involucrata.* A low-growing, sprawling perennial, its single flowers are more of an intense magenta than purple. Its other common name is winecup, aptly. It is a classic rock garden plant, with a deep taproot and a loathing for wet conditions, especially in winter. It blooms from early July into September.

The wisteria arbor was rebuilt in 2008, but the vines haven't missed a beat. Although the showiest species of wisteria hail from Japan and China, there is a local connection that makes it a sweet choice for Chanticleer. The genus is named for Caspar Wistar (1761–1818), who was professor

*In fall, clumps of the aster 'October Skies' tie the terraces together against the russet colors of the grasses.*

*The seventeen steps of varying widths produce a syncopated rhythm to the descent. In June, the upper reaches are decorated with 'Grosso' lavender, milkweed, and the rare Tennessee coneflower.*

of anatomy at the University of Pennsylvania. The author of the genus, the English botanist Thomas Nuttall, first recorded it as *Wisteria,* but later the plant became *Wistaria.* At some point, we returned to the original spelling. There are some interesting contrasts between the Japanese wisteria, *Wisteria floribunda,* and the Chinese species, *W. sinensis.* Floribunda twines clockwise and blooms a little later than its Chinese counterpart. Its racemes tend to be longer and more fragrant but, because they bloom in late April, more veiled by the foliage. The Chinese species twines counterclockwise. The vines here are of the Chinese wisteria cultivar 'Amethyst', introduced for its bright purple coloration and scent. They are smothered in racemes in late April and early May.

It is not the only climber here. Look for the European honeysuckle *Lonicera periclymenum* 'Sweet Sue', selected by the British plantsman Roy Lancaster, a friend of Chanticleer, and named for his wife. Its fragrant cream and yellow flowers appear in late May into June. The arbor also supports the Carolina jessamine, *Gelsemium sempervirens.*

*On the wisteria arbor, a cultivar named 'Amethyst', one of the strongest scented of the Chinese wisterias. The Serpentine can be seen in the background, here planted with the spring flowering rapeseed,* Brassica napus.

*The dainty Tennessee coneflower,* Echinacea tennesseensis, *is a summer staple of the Gravel Garden.*

Donald Wyman once wrote that this fragrant native vine of the South is not hardy north of the southern fringes of coastal Virginia. Hardiness zones have shifted since his day, perhaps due to global warming, and this plant delights visitors in April and May with its profuse and scented yellow trumpets. Nearby grows an unusual buddleja species, *Buddleja lindleyana,* which is actually a suckering shrub but can be trained, with some effort, as a vine. Its violet flower spikes appear in mid-July and just keep growing through the season. By September the base of the panicle consists of ripened seed pods but the tip is still elongating, budding, and flowering. They extend at least twenty-four inches by late summer, at which point Laurel Voran, nervous about the plant seeding, cuts them off.

The arbor path doubles as a viewing platform to observe both the Serpentine and the Pond Garden.

The small, separate rock garden to the right is one of the most enchanting corners of the whole estate; its mounded beds and gravel path invite exploration. The most strik-

*Handmade troughs form a Cubist composition of succulents in chartreuse and blue.*

ing specimens are the three yuccas on the mound. *Yucca rostrata,* commonly the beaked yucca, is admired for its spherical form and fine texture. It is among the yucca species that form a trunk with age, and with time and optimum conditions, the beaked yucca's proud globe sits on a fifteen-foot trunk. It is native to the rocky hills of northern Mexico, and on paper, at least, marginally hardy in southeast Pennsylvania. As with many plants in the Gravel Garden, they have proven quite hardy because of the excellent drainage. The soil was heavily amended when the garden was built and, over the years, expanded. It consists of one-third gravel, one-third sand, and one-third original clay loam.

Look closely at the beaked yucca: the leaves have a blue cast with thin yellow margins. The individual leaves tend to twist, and the globe becomes a study in light and shadow. Its dried fruit is beaked, hence the common name, although these yuccas, planted in 2002, have yet to flower.

Yuccas provide great horticultural theater but are not plants you want to cuddle. For that, there are other cheerful rock garden plants in this little enclave. Carpets of hardy ice plant, *Delosperma,* dominate this garden and begin to flower in July when the prickly pear unfurls its glorious yellow blossom but are still in bloom weeks later when the cactus is merely fruiting. *Delosperma cooperi* has showy two-inch flowers of vivid magenta. *D.* 'Ruby Stars' is—no surprise—smothered in small ruby-red daisies.

Another jewel in this bed is the California-fuchsia, *Zauschneria californica,* with inch-long red tubular flowers borne in abundance in mid- to late summer. It is in bloom well into the fall, allowing hummingbirds to fuel up before heading south for the winter. One of its common names is the hummingbird-fuchsia, although this perennial is related to the evening primrose and is found in California on rocky slopes.

## SPOROBOLUS HILLSIDE

The plant list for the Sporobolus Hillside below the Ruin records eleven woody or herbaceous species, but it is one alone that defines this space. The prairie dropseed, *Sporobolus heterolepis,* is a dry meadow grass, indigenous to the North American prairies, and grows not much more than two feet high and across. It is, simply put, perhaps the most attractive of all native grasses. Finely textured and a deep glossy green, it looks fresh in the heat of June and July, and then puts out silvery panicles on three-foot stems. The inflorescences perfume the air with the scent of coriander. This hillside used to be a lawn in poor heavy clay soil. The soil is still a challenge, but you wouldn't know it by looking at the dropseed.

The grass has a graceful mounding habit. Used en masse, as they are here, they form a meadow that is greater than the sum of its parts. The thousands of clumps take on an abstract but palpable effect of churning water, like a pond in a gale.

By late September the color of the meadow begins to change, and by mid-October the lush green hue has turned to a tan-orange. In winter the color progresses to copper brown. In March the gardeners used to cut the previous season's top growth, but in recent years they have enlisted the help of firefighters for a controlled burn. The grasses at the base of the few woody plants are cut to avoid scorching them. The heat and roar of the fire is scary, but there are ten firefighters and five staff ready with some serious water hoses. After the burn, the meadow looks black and foreboding, and it smells acrid, but soon the grasses come alive, with new shoots pushing through their own soot. When they were simply cut back, they looked like flat-topped clumps at this stage, but now the burnt grasses are tiny mounds, and the new stubble is light gray against the blackened crown. Burning is nature's way of keeping prairies vital—invading woody plants are killed. The fact the grasses have adapted to survive the searing heat makes it no less miraculous. Indeed, they fare better for it. The clumps are rejuvenated and the flowering is showier than when they were cut.

There is another bonus. For a week or two in April, the

*The hillside in autumn, the sporobolus tufts spinning threads of gold beneath the orange foliage of young Japanese cherry trees 'Dream Catcher'.*

meadow looks like a convention of all the world's hedge-hogs.

Near the path to the Ruin, a number of perennials and woody plants dot the fringes of the meadow. 'Fastigiata' is an upright cultivar of the Hinoki false cypress, *Chamaecyparis obtusa,* with attractive dark green fanlike foliage. The coral bark maple, *Acer palmatum* 'Sango kaku', is a handsome small tree, turning a golden yellow in the fall. Alas, its most striking ornament, the vivid pink-red coloration of its youngest branches, occurs in winter during the garden's off-season. Close to the oakleaf drinking fountain, the Chinese honeysuckle, *Lonicera tragophylla,* scrambles over the boulder behind the face rock by Marcia Donahue. The vine is stunning in full bloom; the outer surfaces of the yellow tubular blossoms have a rose blush to them. It is followed by clumps of the purple coneflower cultivar 'Bravado' and the rare New England blazing star, *Liatris scariosa* var. *novae-angliae.*

In the bed behind the retaining wall the gardeners have planted the May-flowering blue wild indigo, *Baptisia australis,* a blue-flowering legume with attractive bluish-green foliage, and another uncommon species of blazing star, *Liatris microcephala,* which flowers later than the common *Liatris spicata,* and from the top down rather than the bottom up. Look for the charming yellow-flowered aster relative, the rosinweed, *Silphium mohrii.* The gardener wants these sporadic plants to look as if they had grown from seed that had blown in.

Four specimens of the upright, pink-flowering cherry 'Dream Catcher' illuminate the hillside in early April, signaling the start of another remarkable year in the heart of Chanticleer Garden.

*After the controlled burn of late winter, the prairie dropseed looks distinctly hedgehog-like.*

# CHAPTER 8

# Cutting Garden

*Long before it became fashionable again to grow your own food, the Cutting Garden was exploring artfully the confluence of a traditional cut-flower and vegetable garden. The Rosengartens had*

always maintained these amenities in parts of the estate, and the present location, open, sunny, and flat, once held an extensive area where fruit, vegetables, herbs, and flowers were grown for the table.

Now smaller in scale, the cutting garden evokes a traditional American cottage garden, especially in summer when the heat invigorates such beauties as annual sunflowers, brilliant dahlias, and crested celosias. By July the intensely planted garden is a playground for hummingbirds, goldfinches, and butterflies and other nectar-sipping insects.

With few woody plants in the mix, the cutting gar-

*Statuesque annuals and perennials add to the exuberant air of the cutting garden beds, here the sunflower variety 'Moulin Rouge'.*

den is the most dynamic part of Chanticleer, and one that builds to harvest season in late August and September. The contrast between its inherent paucity in April to its late-season bounty is simply amazing, and dispels the notion that spring is the peak garden season. The themes and annuals change from year to year, but there are aspects of the garden that return and provide a comforting familiarity. None is sweeter than the hedge of asparagus rising from a long mounded strip that runs the entire length of the garden, broken up by two cross paths. It is the perfect plant, forming a hedge that veils and frames the garden, but with an airiness bestowed by fine texture of its foliage. If it had been a row of raspberry canes or black currants, it would have formed a far heavier and messier barrier.

Gardener Doug Croft keeps a keen eye on the bed in spring, hoping to spot the first shoot to break the mulch. In a normal year the spears appear just as the tulips begin to fade. The purple and green stalks grow in number and length by the day, stretching by as much as four inches between dawns. As fresh spears appear, the asparagus crop is harvested over the following six weeks. No one working at Chanticleer lacks for fresh asparagus in May. By late June the feathery foliage reaches to four feet or more and is left for its ornament and to feed the crowns. Its season comes to a glorious end in October, when the foliage turns golden yellow.

Like hollies, asparagus is dioecious, meaning some plants produce only male flowers, others just female flowers. Many gardeners prefer to use male asparagus plants alone on the grounds that they are larger and more productive. The female plants, however, produce attractive (if seedy) red berries that might be worth the smaller crop. No berries here, though; the bed is planted with the popular staminate cultivar 'Jersey Knight', universally grown for its vigor and disease resistance.

Another permanence is found in the hardy perennials, particularly on the western side of the garden farthest from the vegetable garden. The players include lily of the valley, whose nodding bells are impossibly fragrant. At this latitude, the foliage declines in high summer; like the foxgloves and the bearded irises, it's very much a spring treat. Next to it, Doug Croft grows herbaceous peonies. Seven varieties inhabit this bed, including some lovely single varieties, which are so much less prone to flopping or failing in bud than the top-heavy doubled varieties. 'Krinkled White' is a large semidouble with white ruffled petals around a conspicuous golden boss of anthers. 'Moonstone' is similar, but a creamy light yellow color. 'Sea Shell' is a cupped, single pink, robust and fragrant. It is one of the classic peonies for cutting.

Other flowers of late spring and early summer include two yarrows, the clear yellow-blooming 'Martina' and the soft, earthy reds of 'Terra Cotta'. The adjoining bed features the same varieties of yarrow and a third, 'Lavender Deb', a low-growing lavender-pink selection. The fern at the other end of the bed is a row of the autumn fern, the semievergreen *Dryopteris erythrosora*. What an imaginative inclusion for a cutting garden. In spring the young fronds have a bronze cast to them, and the lower leaf spores are conspicuously red.

Members of the composite family make wonderful cut flowers because the vase life is so long. The hardy daisy in all its forms is well represented in the cutting beds, from asters to rudbeckias, *Helianthus* to coneflowers. One of the most dazzling in August is the tall, multibranched *Rudbeckia subtomentosa* 'Henry Eilers', noted for its tubular rays of orange-yellow radiating from a dark disk. *Helianthus maximilianii* 'Sante Fe' is a perennial sunflower that forms a large clump that is covered in golden bloom in fall.

The garden begins to take on some height with the foxgloves in May and the hollyhocks of June, but a series of arches gives structure even in the bareness of early spring. Fashioned from rebar and driftwood, the ten arches support everything from fleeting tropical vines to the weeping form of the blue atlas cedar, *Cedrus atlantica* 'Pendula'. This is an exceedingly slow-growing form, but in time the needle clusters will hang in a loose veil.

The arches also support a range of clematis varieties chosen for their cutting qualities. 'The President' is a classic six-inch purple-blooming clematis of late spring, valued for its repeat blooming. The gardeners grow a sport of it, 'Multi Blue', whose outer tepals surround a thistle-like cluster of tiny inner tepals. 'Huldine' is another long-favored cultivar, creamy white and slightly cupped. No clematis cutting garden would be complete without 'Henryi', which produces beautifully formed eight-inch white blooms in late spring, and repeats. Its anthers form a conspicuous chocolate brown center. 'Niobe' has deep plum

tepals around golden anthers and is widely loved for its free-flowering habit and long season of bloom.

Dahlias are an important component, though the varieties change from year to year. One of Doug Croft's favorites is 'Sunshine', a bright yellow mignon type, with a red center. The foliage and stems are dark purple. He also likes to use dahlias in the Karma series, which have been bred for cutting. They have a long vase life and straight stems. 'Karma Corona' is a cactus type whose petals are yellow but topped a bronze orange. 'Karma Serena', a decorative form, is heavily double-flowered in a creamy white with a glow of yellow-green in the center. 'Karma Naomi' is another decorative type, a rich mahogany red. 'Karma Prospero' is a lovely soft lilac dahlia, and 'Karma Fuchsiana', as its name suggests, is a glowing magenta. 'Karma Sangria' is another cactus type, but a bicolor of salmon-pink at the petal tops and yellow-green below.

In late summer, amaranth, or, if you prefer, love-lies-bleeding, also plays a key role in providing interest and

*The beds are given character with rustic arches that direct the visitor to the vegetable garden.*

presence in the cutting beds. Varieties have included the 'Emerald Tassels', whose blooms are lime green and great for fall arrangements, and 'Hot Biscuits', grown for its upright plumes the color of cinnamon.

The cold frames play a vital role in the life of this garden. The rear frames in particular are needed to get a jump on the two seasons that occur between February and May. Huh, you ask? Cool-season veggies such as salad greens, beets, and brassicas can be started in the frames in late winter for setting out in April. Warm-season varieties such as tomatoes, sweet basil, cucurbits, and peppers can be sown under glass in early spring for planting out in May after the soil has warmed and frost is but a memory. The frames are inhabited by a toad that takes care of the slugs.

The front frames are used more as a growing area. There is a certain whimsy and artfulness to the way the vegetables are treated and grown, both in the frames and the potager. Doug Croft is happy to let things like mustard

*In a garden that reaches new heights as the season progresses, the strange flowers of the tender vine* Thunbergia gregorii *appear in masses in late summer.*

greens, beets, or lettuces bolt. Suddenly we discover that the dainty, starlike radish blossom is beautiful. And then the seed pod elongates and swells and we learn where we get our seeds from. Indeed, the rat-tailed radish is a selection grown for its edible pods. Doug Croft likes to let arugula run its course. "The white flowers are also edible and are a nice topping and flavor for salads," he says. I once let the biennial root vegetable salsify go to flower and encountered one of the most unusual and attractive blossoms I had seen, lavender and daisylike.

The potager or kitchen garden itself is bounded by lovely, rustic paling, and apart from the perennials like rhubarb and the hardy kiwi vine, the plantings change seasonally and from year to year. Indeed, even the bed layout may change from something strictly rectilinear to curving designs. Once, Croft fashioned pea trellises to match the arching beds, and with their bending wooden frames and taut strings they called to mind ancient, even mythic lyres.

*Visitors find tomatoes and other fruit and vegetables grown as much for their ornament as their flavor.*

Ten weeks after the pea harvest, the trellises were heavy with black-podded beans.

The fence pickets serve to support vines. One year a cherry tomato was patiently woven between the pales as it grew and as Croft removed the suckers in the leaf axils. Often, however, the gardener goes to town with strange cucurbits, once with the honeydew melon 'Snow Leopard', a pale yellow with dark green stripes. It is highly novel variegated cultivar, but if you want to grow it, reach deep. It sells in some catalogs for more than a dollar a seed. You might also find bizarre winter squash growing on the fence, such as the Japanese variety 'Red Kuri'. By September the vine has produced bright orange-red fruit, teardrop-shaped and close to ten pounds in weight. Vegetables, it turns out, are not just trendy again, they have never been more beautiful.

*An unpainted, sun bleached paling fence sets the playful, folksy tone of the vegetable garden.*

# CHAPTER 9

# Parking Lot Garden

*The moment visitors arrive through the Chanticleer gate, the tone is set. This is no ordinary parking lot. It is an elegant space, from the geometry of the entrance circle to the high design of the lot*

itself, with spaces delineated not with paint, but with Belgian block. One is also struck by the idea that this isn't just a car park, it's a garden. Woody plants predominate and the pitch is kept low, but this is an attractive and dynamic landscape, and instructive too. What is not as obvious, given the seamlessness of its design, is that this is wholly a product of Chanticleer the public garden and didn't exist until the early 1990s. In fact, the site didn't even belong to Chanticleer. The property line ran along the left or west side of the entrance driveway, and the lot itself was formerly a neighbor's house, which sat on a grassy hill.

After purchasing the property, the Chanticleer Foun-

*The season's last hurrah of the smooth hydrangea 'Annabelle', gorgeous to the end. The native perennial is planted at the feet of Euonymus hamiltonianus.*

dation set its plan into motion. The house was demolished and the land regraded and retained by a series of walls that vary in scale from relatively modest tapering abutments to the curving wall, some twelve feet high, supporting the entrance circle itself.

The change in elevation dictated the construction of a series of parking levels, but the mass of the lot is more definitively broken up by the placement of the plant beds around the ramps and sublots, which would become richly vegetated. "It was the clear objective from day one that from the moment you turned off Church Road, the experience began in your car, not when you walked through the entrance," said landscape architect Mara Baird, who collaborated with landscape architect Rodney Robinson on the project.

The upper levels, in particular, are screened in a way that is thick but not oppressive, using mostly *Cryptomeria japonica* 'Yoshino' along with some incense cedar and Leyland cypress. Although screening is a major purpose of the

planting scheme throughout the lot, the trees and shrubs are staggered, avoiding the walling effect of big plants set in a row.

On a more human level, the upper lot features a stand of purple smokebush seedlings, *Cotinus coggygria* Purpureus Group. Its members are variously coppiced every other winter, which yields larger leaves but no flowers and keeps the shrub a manageable size. The long ramp from the upper lots to the lower is essentially a mixed border that comes alive in the spring with the flowering of the *Deutzia gracilis* 'Nikko', a wonderful compact mounding shrub whose swelling buds provide almost as much ornament as the flowers in April. This is the moment the large evergreen viburnum, *V. × pragense,* is smothered in white blossoms, and the *Euphorbia amygdaloides* var. *robbiae* is full of acid-green flowers or, actually, long-lived bracts. *Amygdaloides* is botanical Latin for almondlike, and describes the flower, but I prefer one of its common names, Mrs. Robb's Bonnet. This evergreen spurge spreads by rhizomes, quite quickly

*The parking lot garden was designed to show what can be done at a reduced level of maintenance, but the message seems deliciously lost in the frisson of spring.*

in rich, moist soil, more slowly in poorer ground. But once established it makes for a wonderful ground cover in the hardest of situations: dry shade. One of the aims of the Parking Lot Garden is to demonstrate that if you choose the right plants, you can have a beautiful landscape with modest maintenance needs. In recent years, Chanticleer's executive director, Bill Thomas, has taken out some of the fussier and invasive plants to reinforce that message. The gardeners have removed miscanthus grass, landscape roses, mahonia, astilbes, and gooseneck loosestrife, to name a few.

In late summer the ramp border becomes a lovely study in yellows, blues, and purples, with the grouping of *Agastache* 'Purple Haze' with blue false indigo and the showy gray-green lamb's ears 'Helene von Stein'. On the opposing border, the scene is of leadwort bursting into blue flower, and the fading of garden phlox and the purple coneflower. Here too is joe pye weed, *Caryopteris*, and goldenrod. Elsewhere the diminutive, floriferous golden-rod 'Fireworks' is paired with the beautyberry, *Callicarpa dichotoma,* cherished for its clusters of bright purple fruit.

In the lower part of the upper lot, a magnificent specimen of the red buckeye, *Aesculus pavia,* flowers in May. Its ankles are hidden by a massed planting of the suckering shrub *Sorbaria sorbifolia.* It's a coarse plant and not for small gardens, but perfect for utilitarian use like this.

In the lower lot, a pair of handsome zelkovas ('Village Green') are spreading in early maturity, and the one on the right is underplanted with a massing of the smooth hydrangea 'Annabelle', every flower arranger's dream plant. Its brilliant white blooms of August spend the next month aging first to green and then tan.

In the bus lot area, pines are given their due, both the lovely Himalayan pine and the native loblolly, at its northern range here and paired with the staghorn sumac. The latter got too big for its boots, so the gardeners have been cutting it back hard, or much of it, and it returns from suckers. Needless to say, the orange and red fall display of

*Who needs flowers? In decline, the garden takes on a new life of hues and shapes, here provided by the staghorn sumac, feather reed grass, and the zelkova tree.*

*The upright arching beauty of the zelkova is highlighted by snow.*

the sumac against the constant gray-green of the pines is something special.

A Chinese pistache tree, similarly stunning in its orange and red fall foliage, grows near clumps of yellow-twigged dogwood. The latter provide the gardeners with golden stems in winter. They are added to early spring containers that need height, and in recent years they have been used to create an arching fence around the Teacup Garden's central bed—a fence that sprouts and even flowers.

One of the special plants in the Parking Lot Garden is a small deciduous tree, *Euonymus hamiltonianus.* By late August its pendent, balloonlike seedpods open to reveal orange-red seeds surrounded by a fleshy casing (an aril, in garden-speak) that is decidedly magenta. Some may find the color combination clashing, but the plant doesn't seem to care, being more interested in drawing birds to disperse its progeny.

The beds in the entrance circle deserve scrutiny. The simple but powerful pairing in the central bed, of dawn redwoods with *Amsonia hubrichtii,* is one of the signature moments at Chanticleer. The amsonia has its pretty azure astral blooms in the spring, fleeting in an early heat wave, but it is the fall leaf color that makes this feathery perennial so useful, and of course here, with the deciduous conifer, the combination is a stroke of genius. By late October the redwood needles are a brilliant orange, the amsonia's leaves a golden yellow.

The curving bed of the entrance garden has a lot going on. The small tree anchoring the right side is the Dahurian buckthorn, *Rhamnus davurica*. The border is liberally planted with ninebark, and the seasonal and annual plantings might include agaves, *Verbena bonariensis,* flowering tobacco, and the lovely red and white bicolored salvia 'Hot Lips'. Perennials include more of the big-leafed, nonflowering, and heat-tolerant lamb's ears 'Helene von Stein' and *Sedum telephium* 'Matrona', which stonecrop fans value more than the ubiquitous 'Autumn Joy' for its upright form, fleshier leaf, and conspicuous purple stems.

Access to the entrance from the lower lots takes you past the border at the base of the entry circle wall, and here are some lovely plants to savor. My favorite is the purple-flowering giant redbud, *Cercis gigantea*. A month after flowering, the trunks and branches are festooned with shiny red-purple pea pods, whose seeds are sterile. "It frustrates the propagators," said Thomas, "but makes the gardeners happy."

*Even in the utilitarian border of the entrance circle visitors find inspiration for their own gardens.*

CHANTICLEER

————————————

The text of this book is set in Adobe Garamond with
display in Sackers Gothic, Throhandink, and Lamar Pen.